Steam'n Mash!™

Think Fresh. Think Delicious.

Recipes for Every Day of the Week!

AMY MERYDITH

Pascoe Publishing, Inc.

Rockin, California

Published in the United States of America by

Pascoe Publishing, Inc.

Rocklin, California

www.pascoepublishing.com

ISBN: 1-929862-43-1

04 05 06   10 9 8 7 6 5 4 3 2 1

Printed in China

Book Design: Peri Poloni, Knockout Books

Table of Contents

Steam 'n Mash™ Tips

I s there anything more satisfying than the inviting taste of homemade mashed potatoes? What about a slice of spicy pumpkin pie? Or, chunky applesauce eaten while still warm? If you can close your eyes and imagine any of these delicious flavors, the Steam 'n Mash™ was created for you.

In our hurry-up world of time commitments, it is especially enjoyable to hold a bowl of buttery potatoes, sip a thick, creamy soup or taste the tender-crisp vegetables prepared in the Steam 'n Mash™, knowing that you have used fresh produce, herbs and other healthful ingredients to prepare good-for-you meals. These delicious dishes don't have to be prepared in a rush and consumed in 5 minutes. They are packed with nutrients and flavor simply because they are cooked using one of the most ancient forms of heat known to man—steam.

Why is steaming a good way to prepare your food? When heated, water is the perfect conductor for cooking because water adds moisture to foods so that foods are softened as they cook. The moist heat method of cooking can break down tough connective tissue in meat and thick fibrous vegetables. However, foods cooked directly in water lose essential vitamins and minerals. So, your Steam 'n Mash™ provides the answer—moist, gentle heat for optimal nutrition and flavor. Vegetables, fruit, seafood and meats are cooked to tenderness in your Steam 'n Mash™, but do not lose the same amount of nutrients as they do when exposed to liquid and high heat.

I love using my Steam 'n Mash™ for many reasons, but one of the best is that it prepares my food without constant supervision or attention on my part. I can work in the kitchen to prepare the rest of my meal or I can take a break while my food steams and I can relax, knowing that my Steam 'n Mash™ doesn't require hand-holding to bring my dishes to perfect completion. Additionally, I don't need a large pot for cooking, a colander for straining, an electric mixer for mashing and all of the related pieces of equipment that are typically used to make my favorite dishes.

Inside the pages of this book, you will find a wide variety of recipes that are steamed or steamed and mashed using the Steam 'n Mash™. In addition to several variations of mashed potatoes, you will be amazed at the wealth of delicious dishes that you can create in your Steam 'n Mash™ machine! For a wonderful start to any meal, try *Ruby Vegetable Spread* over thin slices of smoked turkey. You will discover new family favorites in *Hearty Lentil & Wild Rice Soup, Fresh Seafood Bisque,* and *Fresh Steamed Asparagus with Lemon Aioli & Slivered Almonds.* Entrées are easy when you prepare *Swiss Chicken Breasts* or *Florentine Flank Steak.* Add a finishing touch for dessert with *Coco Loco Cake* or *Sweet Peaches Ice Cream.* Meals can be truly special when you add even one delicious, yet simple-to-prepare dish to the menu.

When using the Steam 'n Mash™, I have discovered several tips to make food preparation easy. Keep the following in mind for great results every time:

🍴 You will get the best-tasting results from your Steam 'n Mash™ and these recipes when you use fresh ingredients. Choose ripe vegetables and fruit that are free of blemishes and at the peak of freshness. Choose recipes based on which vegetables and fruit are in season and readily available.

¶¶ To peel or not to peel? When steaming and mashing, you may choose to leave the peels on thin-skinned potatoes, such as new red potatoes. The best "mashers," such as Idaho, Russet, Yukon Gold and others are best when peeled prior to steaming and mashing. Remove the eyes from potatoes as much as possible before steaming and avoid using potatoes that have sprouted or become wrinkled during storage. Carrots, some types of squash, and other vegetables and fruit may be steamed and mashed with or without peeling—depending on the recipe you are following and your own preferences.

¶¶ The Steam 'n Mash™ food tray is designed to hold a generous amount of food. Optimally, you will want to steam and mash 2 to 3 pounds of potatoes or other vegetables or fruit at a time. However, when steaming and mashing small amounts of food, you may need to continue using the mix button to pulse the food after the mashing cycle is finished. Unlock the lid and use a spatula to incorporate the food, re-lock the lid and pulse for 30 seconds as needed.

¶¶ To save time during a busy week, double the amount of potatoes you need for your recipe and save the remaining potatoes in an airtight container in the refrigerator. Make potato pancakes, breads, or any of your favorite recipes with the stored potatoes. Use the potatoes within 4 days for best results.

¶¶ Because the steam in your Steam 'n Mash™ is very hot, use potholders when lifting the lid and open the lid away from your face when the cycle is done.

Steam 'n Mash™! ∞ *Think Fresh. Think Delicious.*

¶¶¶ An easy way to prepare very nutritious vegetables is to steam them in the Steam 'n Mash™ according to the Vegetable Chart in the owner's manual. Add a light dash of lemon juice, sea salt and pepper and serve immediately.

¶¶¶ Vegetables should be tender-crisp when done. Set the timer to the shortest steaming time and check the vegetables. Continue steaming if needed. Vegetables will be optimally nutritious when they are tender yet still slightly crisp; not soggy or completely soft.

¶¶¶ Your Steam 'n Mash™ offers the convenience of a "one-dish dinner" appliance. Layer fresh vegetables and chicken or fish of your choice in the food tray. Steam according to the owner's manual suggested cooking times. Remove the food to individual plates and splash each serving with a small amount of soy sauce or flavored-cooking sauce. Add salt and pepper to taste and serve.

¶¶¶

Inviting Sauces, Soufflés & Spreads

Your Steam 'n Mash™ is the perfect companion to create a wide array of sauces, dips, soufflés and spreads. Whether the occasion is a simple evening appetizer or an important dinner party, it is especially welcoming to offer delicious and unique spreads and soufflés for your family and guests. Try *Curried Carrot Pâté* as a delicious starter to a meal of Tandoori Chicken and Jasmine Rice. Bring *Sharp Cheddar & Fuji Apple Spread* to the party and surround with sesame wafers or thin slices of rye bread. The winsome combination of apples and cheddar will delight every guest. For an easy at-home treat, prepare *Red Pepper Dip*, which is packed with nutrition and fiery flavor.

One of the best features of your Steam 'n Mash™ is the way in which applesauce is easily prepared. There are literally hundreds of varieties of apples to choose from when preparing applesauce, so select the flavors you like best—tart, sweet, tangy, or crisp—and steam the apples to perfection. It is very easy to use your Steam 'n Mash™ to prepare applesauce from start to finish. Follow the owner's manual directions and look for the recipes in this chapter, including *At Home Applesauce, Braeburn Apple Sauce,* and *Cinnamon CranApple Sauce* to make the best of this popular fruit.

At Home Applesauce

Prepare this delicious applesauce for a warm dessert over ice cream or vanilla-flavored frozen yogurt.

2 pounds	Granny Smith apples, peeled, cored and quartered (substitute any baking apple, if desired)
1 tablespoon	fresh squeezed lemon juice
1/4 cup	sugar
2 teaspoons	ground cinnamon
1/2 teaspoon	ground allspice

Following the owner's manual directions, attach the mixing arm and place the apples in the food tray. Set the timer to steam and automatic mash for 35-40 minutes or until the apples are tender.

When the mashing cycle ends, add the lemon juice, sugar, cinnamon and allspice. Use the mix button to pulse until blended, about 45 seconds. The applesauce may be tightly covered and refrigerated for up to 1 week.

Makes 10 servings.

Ψ❘Ƿ

Calories 49   Total Fat <1 g.   Saturated Fat <1 g.   % Calories from Fat 5
Carbohydrates 11 g.   Protein <1 g.   Cholesterol 0 mg.   Sodium 3 mg.

Perfectly Pure Baby Applesauce

*A very smooth and pure applesauce—without any
added sugar or spices.*

**6 medium   Gala apples, peeled, cored and quartered
(substitute any baking apple, if desired)**

water as needed

Following the owner's manual directions, attach the mixing arm and
place the apples in the food tray. Set the timer to steam and automatic
mash for 45 minutes or until the apples are tender. When the mashing
cycle ends, add 1-2 tablespoons of water. Use the mix button to pulse
until the texture of the applesauce is uniform.

For a more smooth consistency, transfer the sauce to a blender
and blend on high speed. This is the perfect applesauce for baking
and for baby. The applesauce may be tightly covered and kept in the
refrigerator for up to 1 week.

Makes 6 servings.

⫙⏽

*Calories 81   Total Fat <1 g.   Saturated Fat <1 g.   % Calories from Fat 5
Carbohydrates 21 g.   Protein <1 g.   Cholesterol 0 mg.   Sodium 0 mg.*

Braeburn Apple Sauce

Yams and Braeburn apples combine to create a unique.
golden-colored applesauce. Try this partnered with
pound cake or ice cream.

2	yams, peeled and cubed
5 large	Braeburn apples, peeled, cored and halved (substitute any baking apple, if desired)
1/4 cup	butter or margarine, room temperature
1/2 cup	apple cider
3 tablespoons	light brown sugar
1 teaspoon	salt
1/4 teaspoon	ground white pepper

Following the owner's manual directions, attach the mixing arm and place the yams and apples in the food tray. Set the timer to steam and automatic mash for 40-45 minutes or until the yams are tender.

When the mashing cycle ends, add the butter, cider, brown sugar, salt and pepper. Use the mix button for 1 minute until blended. The sauce will be chunky.

Keep the applesauce tightly covered in the refrigerator for up to 1 week.

Makes 6 to 8 servings.

🍴

Calories 226   Total Fat 6 g.   Saturated Fat 4 g.   % Calories from Fat 23
Carbohydrates 44 g.   Protein 2 g.   Cholesterol 15 mg.   Sodium 35 mg.

Cinnamon CranApple Sauce

Perfect for a dessert, snack or salad—or anything in-between!

6	Fuji apples, peeled and cored
1/4 cup	dark brown sugar
2 teaspoons	ground cinnamon
1 cup	cranberry juice
	ground cinnamon for garnish
	chopped walnuts for garnish

Following the owner's manual directions, attach the mixing arm and place the apples in the food tray. Set the timer to steam and automatic mash for 35-40 minutes or until the apples are tender. When the mashing cycle ends, add the brown sugar and cinnamon. Use the mix button to pulse for 1 minute.

Transfer the sauce to a medium saucepan and add the cranberry juice. Cook over medium heat until the cranapple sauce begins to bubble. Stir and simmer for 5 minutes. To serve, spoon into individual bowls and sprinkle each with a dash of cinnamon and chopped walnuts.

The sauce may be served warm or cold. To store any remaining cranapple sauce, cover tightly and refrigerate for up to 2 weeks.

Makes 6 servings.

⍦❘❘

Calories 185 Total Fat <1 g. Saturated Fat <1 g. % Calories from Fat 4
Carbohydrates 48 g. Protein <1 g. Cholesterol 0 mg. Sodium 10 mg.

Curried Carrot Pâté

This sophisticated spread is especially good for cocktail parties and casual events. Serve with specialty breads or crackers.

3 medium	carrots, peeled and halved
1 tablespoon	extra virgin olive oil
1 small	sweet onion, finely chopped
1/4 cup	water
1/3 cup	fresh squeezed orange juice
1/2 teaspoon	salt
1/4 teaspoon	ground black pepper
1/8 teaspoon	curry powder
1 tablespoon	dry mustard
2 tablespoons	plain nonfat yogurt

Following the owner's manual directions, attach the mixing arm and place the carrots in the food tray. Set the timer to steam and automatic mash for 50 minutes or until the carrots are tender.

In a sauté pan over medium heat, cook the onion in the olive oil until transparent. Reduce the heat to low and add the water, orange juice, salt, pepper, curry and mustard. Bring the liquid to a simmer. When the mashing cycle ends, add the spices, juice and onion to the carrots. Use the mix button to blend for 1 minute. Add the yogurt to the carrots and mix again for 30 seconds. Spoon the pâté into a bowl, cover and refrigerate overnight.

To serve, unmold the pâté onto a serving platter and surround it with cracker bread and fresh vegetables.

Serves 10.

❦

Calories 31 Total Fat 2 g. Saturated Fat <1 g. % Calories from Fat 46
Carbohydrates 4 g. Protein <1 g. Cholesterol <1 mg. Sodium 125 mg.

Ruby Vegetable Spread

*Carrots and beets develop into a rich, earthy spread
that comes to life as an appetizer or casual first course.*

2 small	carrots, peeled and halved
2 small	beets, peeled and quartered
1 tablespoon	extra virgin olive oil
2	shallots, finely chopped
1 cup	white mushrooms, finely chopped
1/2 cup	pecans, chopped
2 tablespoons	fresh parsley, chopped fine
1/4 teaspoon	ground nutmeg
1/8 teaspoon	ground cinnamon
1/2 teaspoon	salt
1/4 teaspoon	ground black pepper

Following the owner's manual directions, attach the mixing arm and place the carrots and beets in the food tray. Set the timer to steam and automatic mash for 50 minutes or until the vegetables are tender.

In a small sauté pan over medium heat, cook the shallots in the oil until soft. Add the mushrooms and the pecans and continue stirring and sautéing until the nuts are toasted. When the mashing cycle ends, add the mushrooms, parsley, nutmeg, cinnamon, salt and pepper. Use the mix button to blend the vegetables until smooth. Transfer the spread to a medium serving bowl and cover. Refrigerate until chilled, at least 2 hours. Serve with thin slices of dark rye bread.

Serves 12.

Calories 58 Total Fat 5 g. Saturated Fat 1 g. % Calories from Fat 71
Carbohydrates 3 g. Protein 1 g. Cholesterol 0 mg. Sodium 111 mg.

Carrot Pudding with Crispy Bacon

*Although Americans may view pudding as "dessert," this pudding
is more adaptive to the European custom of flavored vegetables
with herbs or other light flavors as a light first course.
Well worth the preparation!*

10 medium	carrots, peeled and halved
8 small slices	Canadian bacon
4 large	eggs
1½ cups	light cream or milk
1 cup	smoked cheddar cheese, shredded
1 cup	buttery cracker crumbs, crushed
2 tablespoons	butter or margarine, melted
1/4 teaspoon	salt
1/2 teaspoon	ground black pepper

Following the owner's manual directions, attach the mixing arm and place the carrots in the food tray. Set the timer to steam and automatic mash for 50 minutes or until the carrots are tender. Set aside.

In a medium sauté pan over medium-high heat, brown the Canadian bacon until crispy. Place the crisp bacon on paper towels to cool.

Preheat the oven to 350°F. Lightly butter 8 ramekins. In a medium bowl, whisk the eggs until blended. Add the carrots, cream, cheese, cracker crumbs, butter, salt and pepper. Mix well. Spoon the carrot pudding into the prepared ramekins and place them on a baking sheet. Bake for 30 minutes, or until the pudding is lightly browned.

To serve, top each pudding ramekin with 1 slice of the crisp Canadian bacon.

Makes 8 servings.

Calories 338   Total Fat 24 g.   Saturated Fat 10 g.   % Calories from Fat 62
Carbohydrates 17 g.   Protein 15 g.   Cholesterol 172 mg.   Sodium 737 mg.

Quince Apple Butter

A piece of thick-sliced buttermilk bread and quince apple butter makes any morning a perfect morning!

6	Granny Smith apples, peeled, cored and halved
2	quince, peeled, cored and cubed
1½ cups	water
1/2 cup	cider vinegar
1/2 cup	granulated sugar
dash	salt
1 teaspoon	ground cinnamon
1 teaspoon	ground nutmeg
1 teaspoon	ground allspice
	juice from one lemon
1 tablespoon	lemon zest

Following the owner's manual directions, attach the mixing arm and place the apples and quince in the food tray. Set the timer to steam and automatic mash for 35-40 minutes, or until the quince are tender. When the mashing cycle ends, put the mashed fruit through a sieve or grinder and transfer the fruit to a medium saucepan.

In a large saucepan over low heat, add the water, vinegar, sugar, salt, cinnamon, nutmeg, allspice, lemon juice and zest and stir to combine. Cover and cook until the sugar dissolves. Increase the heat to medium, uncover and stir with a wooden spoon until the butter is smooth and thick. Remove from the heat and cool. Spoon the butter into covered containers. Store the butter in the refrigerator for up to 2 weeks.

Makes 24 servings.

Calories 54   Total Fat <1 g.   Saturated Fat <1 g.   % Calories from Fat 4
Carbohydrates 14 g.   Protein <1 g.   Cholesterol 0 mg.   Sodium 7 mg.

Spiced Anjou Pear Butter

*Anjou pears are sweet on the tongue and this butter
makes a lovely accompaniment to thin wedges of apple,
sliced Stilton cheese and other appetizer offerings.*

4	**Anjou pears, peeled, cored and quartered**
2 tablespoons	*Brown Sugar Vanilla Syrup*
1/4 teaspoon	**ground cinnamon**
1/4 teaspoon	**ground nutmeg**
1/2 teaspoon	**ground cardamom**

Following the owner's manual directions, place the pears in the
food tray. Set the timer to steam for 30 minutes, or until the pears
are tender. Remove the steamed pears and place them in a 2-quart
saucepan. Add the *Brown Sugar Vanilla Syrup*, cinnamon, nutmeg
and cardamom and heat until the liquid is warm. Transfer the butter
to a blender and puree until smooth. Return the puree to the saucepan
and cook over medium heat, stirring constantly, for about 10 minutes.
As the pear butter cooks, its consistency will become like thick honey.
Store refrigerated in a covered container for up to 2 weeks.

Makes 20 servings.

Brown Sugar Vanilla Syrup:

1	vanilla bean
1 cup	water
1 cup	dark brown sugar

To make the syrup, split the vanilla bean in half lengthwise. Combine the water and brown sugar in a small saucepan. Cook over medium heat and stir until the sugar dissolves. Using the tip of a paring knife, scrape the seeds out of the pod into the pan. Increase the heat to high and bring the syrup to a boil. Boil for 1 minute, remove from the heat and let cool completely.

Calories 34   Total Fat <1 g.   Saturated Fat <1 g.   % Calories from Fat 4
Carbohydrates 9 g.   Protein <1 g.   Cholesterol 0 mg.   Sodium <1 mg.

Sharp Cheddar & Fuji Apple Spread

*Serve on stone-ground wheat crackers or
thin slices of smoked turkey.*

3 large	Fuji apples, peeled, cored and halved
1½ cups	Neufchatel cheese, room temperature
1½ cups	sharp cheddar cheese, shredded
3 tablespoons	fresh squeezed lemon juice
1/4 cup	red apple, peeled and shredded
1 teaspoon	ground black pepper
1½ tablespoons	fresh basil, minced

Following the owner's manual directions, attach the mixing arm and place the apples in the food tray. Set the timer to steam and automatic mash for 30 minutes, or until the apples are tender. When the mashing cycle ends, transfer the mashed apples to a bowl and refrigerate until cooled.

In a medium mixing bowl, combine the Neufchatel cheese, cheddar cheese, lemon juice and shredded apple. Mix well. Add the cooled, mashed apples, pepper and basil and mix well again. Cover the bowl and chill for 1 hour.

Makes 24 servings.

¶|●

Calories 99   Total Fat 6 g.   Saturated Fat 4 g.   % Calories from Fat 57
Carbohydrates 5 g.   Protein 5 g.   Cholesterol 21 mg.   Sodium 122 mg.

Herbed Cheddar & Asparagus Soufflé

Light and delicately flavored with fresh asparagus and herbs.

1½ pounds	fresh asparagus, trimmed and cut into ½-inch pieces
1 teaspoon	fresh dill, minced
1 teaspoon	fresh basil, minced
1 teaspoon	salt, divided
1/2 teaspoon	ground black pepper
1 cup	lowfat milk
1/2 cup	light cream
2 tablespoons	margarine
3 tablespoons	all-purpose flour
1½ teaspoons	dry mustard
6 large	eggs, separated and at room temperature
2 cups	sharp white cheddar cheese, shredded

Preheat the oven to 375° F. Lightly coat a 2-quart soufflé dish with cooking spray. Set aside.

Following the owner's manual directions, place the asparagus in the food tray and set the timer to steam for 30 minutes or until the asparagus is tender. Place the steamed asparagus in a medium bowl and add the dill, basil and 1/8 teaspoon salt and the pepper. Set aside.

In a medium saucepan over medium-high heat, bring the milk and cream just to a simmer. In a separate saucepan, melt the butter over medium-low heat. Sprinkle the flour and mustard into the butter, whisking constantly. Reduce the heat to low and continue to cook until a paste is formed. Slowly add the hot milk and cream into the butter and flour, whisking constantly until it thickens.

In a small bowl, beat the egg yolks with a fork and slowly add them to the hot milk, beating vigorously. Add the remaining salt and pepper and continue to whisk. Set aside.

In a large mixing bowl, beat the egg whites with an electric mixer on high speed until stiff peaks form. Gently fold the egg whites, cheese, and asparagus into the milk batter. Transfer the fluffy batter to the prepared soufflé dish and place the dish on a baking sheet. Bake 35 to 40 minutes, or until the soufflé is golden brown. Remove from the oven and serve immediately.

Makes 6 servings.

🍴

Calories 362   Total Fat 26 g.   Saturated Fat 13 g.   % Calories from Fat 64
Carbohydrates 12 g.   Protein 21 g.   Cholesterol 269 mg.   Sodium 751 mg.

Summer Squash Soufflé

An excellent way to use fresh-from-the-garden summer squash.

2 tablespoons	butter or margarine, melted
1 cup	bread crumbs
4 cups	summer squash, peeled and cut into 1-inch slices
1 medium	white onion, chopped
1/2 teaspoon	salt
1/2 teaspoon	garlic salt
1/8 teaspoon	ground black pepper
1 cup	light cream
2	eggs, lightly beaten
3 tablespoons	all-purpose flour
1 cup	sharp cheddar cheese, shredded
	buttered bread crumbs for garnish

Preheat the oven to 350°F. Coat a 1½-quart baking dish with cooking spray.

To make the buttered bread crumbs, stir together the melted butter and the bread crumbs. Place on a baking sheet and heat under the broiler just until slightly browned. Watch carefully to avoid burning the crumbs. Set aside.

Following the owner's manual directions, attach the mixing arm and place the summer squash and onion into the food tray. Set the timer to steam and automatic mash for 20 minutes or until the squash is tender. When the mashing cycle ends, add the salt, garlic salt, pepper, cream, eggs, flour and cheese. Use the mix button to pulse until well blended, about 1 minute. Spoon the batter into the prepared baking dish and bake for 30 minutes. Sprinkle the buttered bread crumbs on top of the soufflé and continue baking for another 10 minutes.

Makes 4 servings.

🍴

*Calories 447   Total Fat 27 g.   Saturated Fat 11 g.   % Calories from Fat 53
Carbohydrates 34 g.   Protein 18 g.   Cholesterol 173 mg.   Sodium 949 mg.*

Fresh Herb & Artichoke Soufflé

Artichokes are perfect when steamed to tenderness and the addition of Romano cheese creates a special light entrée or appetizer.

1/4 cup	butter, melted and divided
1/2 cup	toasted pecans, finely chopped and divided
1/2 cup	Romano cheese, freshly grated and divided
1 pound	Jerusalem artichokes, peeled and cubed
1/4 cup	all-purpose flour
2 cups	lowfat milk
1 cup	light cream
4 large	egg yolks
2 teaspoons	salt
1/2 teaspoon	ground black pepper
1½ teaspoons	fresh rosemary, finely chopped
1 teaspoon	fresh thyme, finely chopped
4 large	egg whites, room temperature

Preheat the oven to 400°F. Brush the inside of a 1½-quart soufflé dish with 1 tablespoon of the melted butter. Add 2 tablespoons each of the pecans and Romano cheese, swirling to coat the sides of the dish. Set aside.

Following the owner's manual directions, attach the mixing arm and place the artichokes in the food tray. Set the timer to steam and automatic mash for 45 minutes or until the artichokes are tender. Use the mix button to pulse the artichokes for an additional 30 seconds until the artichokes are pureed.

In a 1-quart saucepan over medium heat, bring the melted butter just to a boil. Whisk in the flour, cooking and stirring for 2 minutes. Slowly add the milk and cream and continue to whisk. Whisk in the artichoke puree and remove the pan from the heat. Add the egg yolks, one at a time, whisking until smooth. Stir in the salt, pepper, herbs and remaining cheese and pecans.

Using an electric mixer, beat the egg whites on high speed until stiff peaks form. Gently fold the egg whites into the batter. Spoon the finished batter into the prepared dish. Bake until the soufflé is puffed and golden brown, about 40 minutes. Serve immediately.

Makes 4 to 6 servings.

🍴

Calories 430   Total Fat 31 g.   Saturated Fat 10 g.   % Calories from Fat 63
Carbohydrates 25 g.   Protein 15 g.   Cholesterol 203 mg.   Sodium 1024 mg.

Golden Carrot Soufflé with Whipped Cream

Try serving reduced-fat ham slices with this soufflé.

2 pounds	carrots, peeled and halved
1/2 cup	sugar, divided
1/4 cup	dark brown sugar
2 tablespoons	all-purpose flour
1½ teaspoons	baking powder
2 teaspoons	vanilla extract
3	eggs, room temperature
3 tablespoons	butter or margarine, softened
1 tablespoon	sugar
	whipped cream and grated carrot for garnish

Following the owner's manual directions, attach the mixing arm and place the carrots in the food tray. Set the timer to steam and automatic mash for 50 minutes or until the carrots are tender.

Preheat oven to 350°F. Lightly coat a 1½-quart soufflé dish with cooking spray and dust the bottom and sides with 1 tablespoon of the sugar. When the mashing cycle ends, add the remaining sugar, brown sugar, flour, baking powder and vanilla to the carrots. Use the mix button to blend well. Add the eggs one at a time, mixing for 10 seconds after each addition. Add the butter and mix for 30 seconds. Spoon the soufflé batter into the prepared dish and bake for 45 minutes, or until the soufflé is set in the center. Remove from the oven and serve immediately.

To serve, spoon individual servings onto plates and top with whipped cream. Garnish with the grated carrot.

Makes 10 servings.

🍴

*Calories 163   Total Fat 5 g.   Saturated Fat 3 g.   % Calories from Fat 28
Carbohydrates 27 g.   Protein 3 g.   Cholesterol 74 mg.   Sodium 113 mg.*

Spiced Apple Soufflé

A soufflé that can be a starter course or a dessert course.
Either way, the tart Granny Smith apples bring tart
and sweet definition to the soufflé.

2 medium	Granny Smith apples, peeled, cored and quartered
2 tablespoons	apple juice
1½ teaspoons	fresh squeezed lemon juice
4	egg yolks
2 tablespoons	butter or margarine
3 tablespoons	all-purpose flour
1 cup	light cream
4	egg whites
1 teaspoon	vanilla extract
1/4 cup	sugar
pinch	ground cinnamon for garnish

Following the owner's manual direction, attach the mixing arm and place the apples in the food tray. Set the timer to steam and automatic mash for 30 minutes or until the apples are tender. When the mashing cycle ends, add the apple juice and lemon juice to the mashed apples. Use the mix button to blend for 45 seconds. Set aside.

Preheat the oven to 350°F. Lightly butter the bottom and sides of a 1½-quart soufflé dish. Sprinkle with sugar to cover and set aside. In a medium mixing bowl, beat the egg yolks. Melt the butter in a small saucepan over low heat. Stir in the flour until smooth and add the cream. Cook over medium heat until thick and bubbly, stirring constantly. Remove from the heat and add to the beaten egg yolks. Add the apple mixture to the batter and stir to blend.

In a deep mixing bowl, beat the egg whites and vanilla with an electric mixer on high speed until soft peaks form. Gradually add the sugar one tablespoon at a time, until stiff glossy peaks form. Gently fold the batter into the egg whites. Carefully transfer the batter to the soufflé dish and bake for 35 minutes or until a toothpick inserted in the center comes out clean. Serve immediately. Sprinkle cinnamon on the top of each serving.

Makes 6 servings.

🍴

Calories 241   Total Fat 15 g.   Saturated Fat 8 g.   % Calories from Fat 56
Carbohydrates 21 g.   Protein 6 g.   Cholesterol 179 mg.   Sodium 61 mg.

Mediterranean Eggplant & Cilantro Dip

A delightful alternative to chips and salsa.

1 large	eggplant, peeled & chopped
2 tablespoons	rosemary-infused olive oil
2 cloves	garlic, minced
15 ounce	can crushed tomatoes
1	red bell pepper, chopped and seeded
1½ teaspoons	ground cumin
1/2 teaspoon	cayenne pepper
1 teaspoon	sugar
	salt to taste
1/4 cup	balsamic vinegar
2 tablespoons	fresh cilantro, minced
2 tablespoons	green onion, minced

Following the owner's manual directions place the eggplant in the food tray and set the timer to steam for 30 minutes, or until the eggplant is tender. Set aside to cool slightly.

In a large sauté pan, heat the oil over medium-high heat. Add the garlic, tomatoes, bell pepper, cumin, cayenne pepper, sugar, salt and vinegar and cook until heated through. Add the steamed eggplant and stir to combine. Cook on high until boiling, stirring constantly for about 5 minutes.

Remove from the heat and pour into a serving bowl. Cover and refrigerate until chilled. To serve, top the dip with the fresh cilantro and onions and serve with chips or wedges of pita bread.

Makes 8 servings.

🍴

Calories 82   Total Fat 4 g.   Saturated Fat 1 g.   % Calories from Fat 41
Carbohydrates 10 g.   Protein 2 g.   Cholesterol 0 mg.   Sodium 86 mg.

Red Pepper Dip

A healthful, spicy dip for any occasion.

1 large	eggplant, peeled and cubed
1 tablespoon	lemon juice
2 cloves	garlic, minced
2 teaspoons	red pepper flakes
1 tablespoon	fresh parsley, chopped
1 teaspoon	sesame seed oil
½ teaspoon	salt

Following the owner's manual directions, attach the mixing arm and place the eggplant into the food tray. Set the timer to steam and automatic mash for 30 minutes, until the eggplant is tender. When the mashing cycle ends, add the lemon juice, garlic, red pepper, parsley, sesame seed oil and salt. Use the mix button to pulse until well blended.

Place the dip in a small bowl, cover and chill. Serve with whole wheat crackers or toasted pita bread.

Makes 6 to 8 servings.

🍴

Calories 25   Total Fat 1 g.   Saturated Fat <1 g.   % Calories from Fat 27
Carbohydrates 4 g.   Protein 1 g.   Cholesterol 0 mg.   Sodium 148 mg.

Chapter Two

Satisfying Soups

There is nothing quite as warm and welcoming as a hearty bowl of soup. And because your Steam 'n Mash™ easily prepares smoothly mashed vegetables, you can create many thick and hearty soups using nutritious vegetables as the starting place instead of butter, cream and flour. Light soups can also be used for a first course and can be served chilled, such as *Russian Beet Borscht with Sour Cream* or *Chilled Bosc Pear Soup.*

Seasonally, you will find fresh vegetables perfect for making soup. Potatoes, zucchini, cauliflower and broccoli may not be "child-friendly" when served alone, but when blended into soups, they can quickly become favorites. Add pasta, rice or chopped meats for a wholesome meal anytime of the year.

When making choices based on healthful living, you will want to substitute lowfat milk, lowfat margarine and fat-reduced cheese in recipes that call for cream or other rich ingredients. You may want to add or delete ingredients according to your own preferences, but don't be afraid to experiment—your Steam 'n Mash™ makes cooking easy!

Italian Sausage & Zucchini Soup

Zesty and garden-fresh!

4	zucchini squash, unpeeled and thinly sliced
2 tablespoons	butter or margarine
1 clove	garlic, minced
1 cup	beefsteak tomatoes, diced
1 teaspoon	fresh oregano, minced
1 teaspoon	fresh basil, minced
1/2 pound	turkey Italian sausage, cooked
3 cups	low-sodium vegetable broth
1/4 cup	Romano cheese, freshly grated

Following the owner's manual directions, place the zucchini in the food tray and steam for 20 minutes or until the zucchini is just tender.

In a stockpot over medium-high heat, melt the butter and sauté the garlic until tender. Add the tomatoes, oregano and basil. Simmer on low heat for 3 minutes, add the sausage and stir to combine. Add the vegetable broth and continue simmering for 5 minutes.

Spoon the steamed zucchini into the soup. Stir occasionally as the soup simmers for 3 minutes.

Ladle the soup into individual bowls and sprinkle with the Romano cheese.

Makes 2 servings.

🍴

Calories 572   Total Fat 19 g.   Saturated Fat 21 g.   % Calories from Fat 32
Carbohydrates 17 g.   Protein 27 g.   Cholesterol 104 mg.   Sodium 1514 mg.

Asiago Potato Soup

Especially inviting on a cold winter's day, the potatoes, ham and Asiago cheese in this recipe will invigorate even the most chilled guest.

1 pound	russet potatoes, peeled and quartered
1 cup	light cream
3 tablespoons	butter or margarine, divided
1/4 cup	white onion, chopped
1 clove	garlic, minced
1 cup	ham, cooked and diced
2 cups	lowfat milk
	salt and pepper to taste
1/2 cup	Asiago cheese, shredded
	fresh parsley for garnish

Following the owner's manual directions, place the potatoes in the food tray and steam for 45 minutes or until the potatoes are tender. In a small saucepan heat the cream just until it steams. Add 2 tablespoons butter and set aside. Attach the mixing arm, drizzle the cream over the potatoes and mix for 10 to 20 seconds. Set aside.

In a large stockpot over medium heat, melt the remaining butter and sauté the onion and garlic until tender. Add the ham and reduce the heat to low. Stir in the mashed potatoes. Slowly stir in the milk. Add the salt and pepper to taste and heat through.

To serve, evenly divide the shredded cheese between four individual soup bowls. Ladle the soup into the bowls and garnish each with fresh parsley.

Makes 4 servings.

Calories 461 Total Fat 34 g. Saturated Fat 15 g. % Calories from Fat 64
Carbohydrates 17 g. Protein 25 g. Cholesterol 94 mg. Sodium 984 mg.

Creamy Cheddar & Broccoli Soup

A great way to incorporate fresh vegetables—broccoli, cauliflower and onion—into your daily diet.

1 small	head broccoli, chopped
1 small	head cauliflower, chopped
1/4 cup	yellow onion, chopped
1 tablespoon	lowfat margarine
1 cup	low-sodium vegetable broth
2 cups	lowfat milk
1 cup	water
1/4 teaspoon	ground allspice
1/2 teaspoon	salt
1/4 teaspoon	ground black pepper
1/2 cup	reduced-fat cheddar cheese, shredded
1 tablespoon	cornstarch (optional)
2 tablespoons	water (optional)

Following the owner's manual directions, attach the mixing arm. Place the broccoli and cauliflower into the food tray and set the timer to steam and automatic mash for 35-40 minutes, or until the vegetables are tender.

In a stockpot over medium-high heat, sauté the onion in the margarine until the onion is soft. Add the vegetable broth, milk and water and stir well to combine. Cook on medium-high until the soup is simmering. Add the mashed broccoli and cauliflower and stir well. Add the allspice, salt, pepper and cheese and continue to cook until the cheese is melted. If the soup is too thin, mix the cornstarch with the water and add to the simmering soup. Stir as the soup thickens.

Makes 8 servings.

✕|❢

Calories 91   Total Fat 2 g.   Saturated Fat 1 g.   % Calories from Fat 21
Carbohydrates 12 g.   Protein 8 g.   Cholesterol 6 mg.   Sodium 333 mg.

Hearty Lentil & Wild Rice Soup

*Steamed lentils provide a thick and smooth base
for this lovely soup.*

1½ cups	canned lentils, rinsed and drained
3 cloves	garlic, peeled
1 teaspoon	salt
2 large	carrots, peeled and sliced
1/3 cup	celery, chopped
1 medium	white onion, chopped
1 tablespoon	extra virgin olive oil
3 14½ ounce	cans chunky tomatoes
1 cup	wild rice, uncooked
7 cups	low-sodium vegetable broth (substitute chicken broth, if desired)
4 cups	water
1 tablespoon	fresh basil, minced
1 tablespoon	fresh thyme, minced
2 tablespoons	fresh parsley, minced
3 drops	hot sauce to taste
1/2 teaspoon	ground black pepper

Following the owner's manual directions, attach the mixing arm and place the lentils and garlic in the food tray. Set the timer to steam and automatic mash for 25 minutes. When the mashing cycle is done, add the salt and mix just until incorporated. Set aside.

In a large stockpot over medium-high heat, sauté the carrots, celery and onion in the oil until the vegetables are tender. Add the tomatoes, rice, broth, water, basil and thyme and mix well. Bring the soup to a boil over medium-high heat, reduce the heat to low and simmer until the rice is tender. Stir occasionally. Add the lentils, parsley, hot sauce and pepper and mix well.

Simmer for an additional 10 minutes and serve with hot whole grain bread.

Makes 10 servings.

🍴

Calories 217 Total Fat 2 g. Saturated Fat <1 g. % Calories from Fat 9 Carbohydrates 39 g. Protein 12 g. Cholesterol 0 mg. Sodium 850 mg.

Russian Beet Borscht with Sour Cream

A classic Russian soup using the earthy richness of beets.

4 medium	whole beets, rinsed and cut in half
2 teaspoons	butter or lowfat margarine
1 cup	leeks, white part only, sliced
1 small	yellow onion, chopped
2 teaspoons	sugar
4 cups	water
2 teaspoons	instant chicken bouillon
1 teaspoon	white vinegar
	salt and pepper to taste
	sour cream and chopped chives for garnish

Following the owner's manual instructions, place the beets in the food tray. Set the timer to steam for 50-60 minutes. When the steaming cycle ends, allow the beets to cool until they are easy to handle. Peel the skin from the beets, cut into coarse chunks and place in the food tray again. Attach the mixing arm and use the mix button to pulse until the beets are pureed. Set aside.

In a large stockpot over medium-high heat, sauté the leeks, onion and sugar in the butter until the sugar caramelizes. Turn the heat to low, add the pureed beets and stir to combine. Slowly add the water, bouillon and vinegar, turn the heat to medium, and bring the soup to a low simmer. Add salt and pepper to taste. Remove the soup from the heat, cool and then chill.

To serve, ladle the soup into individual bowls and top with sour cream and a sprinkling of chives.

Serves 4.

🍴

Calories 90   Total Fat 3 g.   Saturated Fat 1 g.   % Calories from Fat 26
Carbohydrates 16 g.   Protein 2 g.   Cholesterol 8 mg.   Sodium 73 mg.

Fresh Seafood Bisque

This bisque is worthy of the most special occasion.

1/2 pound	uncooked shrimp, cleaned, shelled, deveined
1/3 pound	cod or white fish fillet (one piece)
1/3 pound	salmon fillet (one piece, remove skin)
1/2 cup	shallots, finely chopped
1/4 cup	celery, finely diced
1/2 pound	butter
4 cups	low-sodium fish or chicken broth
2 6½ ounce	cans chopped clams with juice
1/4 teaspoon	white pepper
4 cups	heavy cream
6½ ounce	can crab meat
2 tablespoons	dry sherry
	chives, chopped, for garnish

Following the owner's manual directions, place the shrimp, cod and salmon in the food tray. Set the timer to steam for 15 to 25 minutes until the fish is tender and flakes easily. Cool and remove the skin from the fish. Flake the fish meat.

In a stockpot over medium heat, sauté the shallots and diced celery in the butter until the vegetables are soft. Add the fish or chicken broth and bring to a simmer. Add the clams with their juice and the white pepper. Simmer the soup for 5 minutes. Add the flaked fish, shrimp, crab meat, heavy cream and the dry sherry. Stir gently and bring the bisque to a simmer and heat through. To serve, ladle the bisque into individual bowls and garnish with the chives.

Makes 8-10 servings.

🍴

Calories 615   Total Fat 57 g.   Saturated Fat 34 g.   % Calories from Fat 82
Carbohydrates 7 g.   Protein 19 g.   Cholesterol 260 mg.   Sodium 521 mg.

East Indian Curry Soup

Enjoy the exotic flavors of curry, cayenne pepper and fresh vegetables wrapped up in an inviting soup.

4 medium	carrots, peeled and halved
1 small	zucchini, peeled and sliced thick
1 small	yellow squash, peeled and sliced thick
1 tablespoon	extra virgin olive oil
1 small	sweet onion, chopped
2 cups	low-sodium vegetable broth
1/2 cup	light cream
2 teaspoons	curry powder
1/4 teaspoon	cayenne pepper
1/2 teaspoon	salt
1/4 teaspoon	ground black pepper
	fresh parsley, chopped, for garnish

Following the owner's manual directions, attach the mixing arm and place the carrots, zucchini and squash in the food tray. Set the timer to steam and automatic mash for 35-45 minutes or until the vegetables are tender.

In a large stockpot over medium-high heat, sauté the onion in the olive oil until soft. Reduce the heat to low, add the vegetable broth, cream, curry powder, cayenne pepper, salt and pepper. Bring the soup to a low simmer. Spoon the mashed vegetables into the soup and stir until well blended. Heat and simmer again for 5 minutes.

To serve, ladle the soup into individual bowls and sprinkle with the fresh parsley.

Makes 4 servings.

🍴

*Calories 143   **Total Fat** 10 g.   Saturated Fat 4 g.   % Calories from Fat 60*
*Carbohydrates 12 g.   **Protein** 3 g.   Cholesterol 20 mg.   **Sodium** 550 mg.*

Wintry Apple & Acorn Squash Soup

Apples and squash combine in a sweet-tart, spicy soup.

4	Fuji apples, cored, halved and peeled (substitute any red apples, if desired)
1 small	acorn squash, seeded and quartered
1 small	yellow onion, quartered
1 clove	garlic, peeled
1 tablespoon	butter
4 cups	low-sodium vegetable broth
1 cup	water
1/2 teaspoon	ground ginger
1/2 teaspoon	ground cumin
1/4 teaspoon	ground white pepper
	ground nutmeg for garnish

Following the owner's manual directions, place the apples, squash, onion and garlic in the food tray. Set the timer to steam for 30 to 45 minutes or until the apples and squash are tender. When the steaming cycle ends, remove the squash, spoon the pulp back into the food tray and discard the shell. Attach the mixing arm, add the butter and mash until the apples and vegetables are smooth.

In a large stockpot over medium-high heat, bring the broth and water to a boil. Spoon the mashed apples and vegetables into the broth. Stir well to combine. Add the ginger, cumin and pepper. Heat completely.

To serve, ladle the hot soup into individual bowls and sprinkle with nutmeg.

Makes 6 servings.

♈︎❙♈︎

Calories 143 **Total Fat 3 g.** *Saturated Fat 1 g.* **% Calories from Fat 16**
Carbohydrates 30 g. **Protein 2 g.** *Cholesterol 6 mg.* **Sodium 301 mg.**

Chilled Bosc Pear Soup

Elegant and perfect for a fancy luncheon.

6	Bosc pears, peeled, cored and quartered
2 cups	water
1/2 cup	unsweetened pear juice
1/4 cup	sugar
1 tablespoon	orange zest
1½ teaspoons	fennel seed
	shortbread cookies, crumbled, for garnish
	fresh raspberries for garnish

Following the owner's manual directions, attach the mixing arm and place the pears in the food tray. Set the timer to steam and automatic mash for 45 minutes or until the pears are tender.

In a large stockpot over medium heat, combine the water, juice, sugar, orange zest and fennel seed. Bring to a boil and reduce the heat to low. Simmer for 5 minutes. Strain the liquid and discard the spices. Return the soup to the stockpot. Spoon the mashed pears into the soup broth and simmer for 10 minutes, stirring often. If desired, place the soup in a blender for smoother consistency. Refrigerate the soup until it is chilled.

To serve, ladle the chilled soup into individual bowls. Sprinkle the soup with the crumbled shortbread cookies and a few fresh raspberries.

Makes 6 servings.

ᵚ¦ᵖ

Calories 168   Total Fat 1 g.   Saturated Fat <1 g.   % Calories from Fat 4
Carbohydrates 43 g.   Protein 1 g.   Cholesterol 0 mg.   Sodium 1 mg.

French Leek Soup

Easy to prepare—and easy to enjoy.

4 medium	russet potatoes, peeled and quartered
1/3 cup	lowfat margarine
3 large	leeks, finely chopped
1	celery stalk, finely chopped
3½ cups	low-sodium chicken broth
1 cup	water
1 teaspoon	salt
1/4 teaspoon	ground black pepper
1/2 cup	lowfat milk
sprigs	parsley for garnish

Following the owner's manual directions, attach the mixing arm and place the potatoes in the food tray. Set the timer to steam and automatic mash for 35-40 minutes or until tender.

In a large stockpot over medium-high heat, melt the margarine and add the leeks and celery. Sauté just until the leeks begin to soften. Add the mashed potatoes to the vegetables and combine. Slowly stir in the broth and water, whisking in the potatoes as the liquid is added. Stir in the salt, pepper and milk and blend. Heat to a simmer, but do not boil.

This soup may be served hot or cold. Ladle the soup into individual bowls and top each with a sprig of parsley.

Makes 8 servings.

TŢ

Calories 77   Total Fat 2 g.   Saturated Fat 1 g.   % Calories from Fat 26
Carbohydrates 11 g.   Protein 4 g.   Cholesterol 1 mg.   Sodium 495 mg.

Tuscany Chicken & Vegetable Soup

*Use your Steam 'n Mash™ to steam the chicken for this soup.
Cool and shred the chicken into small pieces.*

1 large	eggplant, peeled and cubed
1	sweet onion, chopped
1	garlic clove, minced
2 tablespoons	extra virgin olive oil
3 to 4 cups	cooked chicken, shredded
2 cups	low-sodium chicken broth
2 cups	water
1	zucchini, sliced thinly
1	carrot, peeled and sliced thinly
6 ounces	thin pasta noodles
	salt and pepper to taste

Following the owner's manual directions attach the mixing arm and place the eggplant into the food tray. Set the timer to steam and mash for 30 minutes, or until the eggplant is tender.

In a large stockpot over medium-high heat, sauté the onion and garlic in the olive oil until soft. Add the shredded chicken, chicken broth and water. Stir and add the mashed eggplant. Stir again and heat to simmering. Add the salt and pepper and simmer for 5 minutes. Add the squash, carrot and noodles. Simmer until the noodles are tender. To serve, ladle the hot soup into individual bowls.

Makes 4 servings.

Calories 459   Total Fat 13 g.   Saturated Fat 3 g.   % Calories from Fat 27
Carbohydrates 41 g.   Protein 42 g.   Cholesterol 138 mg.   Sodium 213 mg.

Chapter Three

Garden-Fresh Vegetables & Salads

G arden vegetables can be a most delicious addition to any meal, but most cooks either undercook or overcook vegetables with unappetizing results. Your Steam 'n Mash™ was designed to perfectly cook your vegetables every time. Steaming brings out the best of vegetables because the vegetables are cooked without a high degree of water absorption and the vegetables consequently remain crisp, yet tender. After you set the timer for your vegetables, all you need to do is relax. Set the timer for 5 minutes prior to the allotted steaming time so that you will not overcook your vegetables. It is always better to underestimate than to overcook the vegetables.

The recipes in this chapter are for any day of the week or for special occasions when you want something special for your family and guests. Try *Steamed Fresh Spinach with Tangerine Vinaigrette* and *Chilled Asparagus Salad with Chardonnay Dressing* for an exciting change of pace. Use vegetables as the base for easy meatless entrées, such as *Ricotta & Spinach-Stuffed Red Peppers.* or *Mini Pumpkins with Swiss Cheese.* And, who could resist *Tri-Pepper Potato Salad* at your next picnic? Enjoy the perfect flavors of nature within these delicious recipes.

Balsamic & Fresh Herb Steamed Veggies

A splash of balsamic vinegar brings these vegetables to life.

6	fresh carrots, peeled and cut into 3-inch chunks
6	whole zucchini, unpeeled, cut into 3-inch chunks
1	purple onion, peeled and cut into 8 pieces
1 cup	crimini mushrooms
2 tablespoons	extra virgin olive oil
2 tablespoons	balsamic vinegar
1/2 teaspoon	sea salt
1/2 teaspoon	freshly ground black pepper
1 teaspoon	fresh basil, minced
1 teaspoon	fresh thyme, minced
1 teaspoon	fresh parsley, minced

Following the owner's manual instructions, place the carrots in the food tray. Set the timer to steam for 30 minutes. When the steaming cycle ends, add the zucchini, onion and mushrooms to the carrots and set the timer to steam for 20-25 minutes, or until all of the vegetables are tender-crisp.

In a small bowl, whisk together the oil and vinegar. Add the salt and pepper and whisk again. Sprinkle the fresh herbs over the oil and vinegar and stir lightly.

Arrange the steamed vegetables on a small serving platter and drizzle the herb dressing over all.

Serves 4.

Calories 177   Total Fat 8 g.   Saturated Fat 1 g.   % Calories from Fat 37
Carbohydrates 25 g.   Protein 6 g.   Cholesterol 0 mg.   Sodium 34 mg.

Chili-Sauced Steamed Cabbage

An unusual twist on typical cabbage dishes.
Serve with corned beef.

2 cups	ripe beefsteak tomatoes, chopped
1/4 cup	yellow bell pepper, diced
1/4 cup	green bell pepper, diced
1/4 cup	sweet red onion, minced
1/4 cup	white vinegar
2 tablespoons	honey
1 teaspoon	chili powder
1/4 teaspoon	dry mustard
1/8 teaspoon	cayenne pepper
2 pounds	red or green cabbage, quartered

In a non-reactive bowl, combine the tomatoes, bell peppers, onion, vinegar, honey, chili powder, dry mustard and cayenne pepper. Cover and refrigerate.

Following the owner's manual instructions, place the cabbage in the food tray. Set the timer to steam for 45-55 minutes or until the cabbage is tender.

To serve, place the cabbage on a platter and spoon the chili sauce over the top. Serve immediately.

Serves 8.

🍴

Calories 62   Total Fat <1 g.   Saturated Fat <1 g.   % Calories from Fat 6
Carbohydrates 15 g.   Protein 2 g.   Cholesterol 0 mg.   Sodium 18 mg.

Ricotta & Spinach-Stuffed Red Peppers

A meatless entrée packed with healthful goodness.

12 ounces	lowfat ricotta cheese
2 cups	fresh spinach, cleaned and chopped
2 teaspoons	fresh basil, chopped
2 teaspoons	fresh Italian parsley, chopped
1/4 cup	black olives, diced
2 whole	red bell peppers, tops removed and cored

In a medium bowl, stir together the ricotta cheese, spinach, basil, parsley and black olives. Divide the stuffing evenly between the two red bell peppers. Following the owner's manual instructions place the bell peppers into the food tray. Set the timer to steam for 30-40 minutes or until the bell peppers are just tender. Remove, cut each pepper in half and serve.

Serves 4.

Calories 151 Total Fat 8 g. Saturated Fat 3 g. % Calories from Fat 50
Carbohydrates 8 g. Protein 10 g. Cholesterol 30 mg. Sodium 280 mg.

Fresh Steamed Asparagus with Lemon Aioli & Slivered Almonds

Choose thin stalks of asparagus for optimal tenderness.

1 pound	fresh asparagus, cleaned, tough ends removed and cut in half
1 teaspoon	fresh lemon juice
2 tablespoons	lowfat mayonnaise
1/4 teaspoon	extra virgin olive oil
1/4 teaspoon	white pepper
3 tablespoons	slivered almonds

Following the owner's manual directions, place the asparagus in the food tray. Set the timer to steam for 30-35 minutes. When the steaming cycle ends, remove the asparagus to a serving platter with a slotted spoon.

Whisk together the lemon juice, mayonnaise, oil and white pepper. Drizzle the aioli over the asparagus and garnish with the slivered almonds.

Serves 3-4.

Calories 71   Total Fat 4 g.   Saturated Fat <1 g.   % Calories from Fat 40
Carbohydrates 8 g.   Protein 4 g.   Cholesterol 0 mg.   Sodium 72 mg.

Steamed Asparagus with Sweet Purple Onions

Colorful and flavorful, partner this vegetable dish with any meat or poultry entrée.

1 pound	fresh asparagus, rinsed and trimmed of woody stems
1	sweet purple onion, sliced into ¼-inch rounds
2 teaspoons	balsamic vinegar
1 tablespoon	extra virgin olive oil
	salt and black pepper to taste
	fresh parsley, chopped, for garnish

Following the owner's manual instructions, place the asparagus spears and red onion slices in the food tray. Set the timer to steam for 30-35 minutes or until the asparagus is just tender.

To serve place the steamed asparagus on a platter and top with the sweet onions. Drizzle the balsamic vinegar and the olive oil over the top of the vegetables. Sprinkle with salt and pepper and top with a garnish of parsley. Serve immediately.

Serves 3-4.

🍴

Calories 75   Total Fat 4 g.   Saturated Fat <1 g.   % Calories from Fat 42
Carbohydrates 9 g.   Protein 3 g.   Cholesterol 0 mg.   Sodium 3 mg.

Steamed Fresh Spinach with Tangerine Vinaigrette

Add canned tangerine segments for additional color and zest, if desired.

1 pound	fresh spinach, washed and torn into large pieces
1/4 cup	dried cranberries

Tangerine Vinaigrette:

3 tablespoons	freshly squeezed tangerine juice
1 tablespoon	sherry
2 teaspoons	tangerine zest
1 small	shallot, minced
pinch	salt
1/4 cup	extra virgin olive oil

Following the owner's manual instructions, place the spinach in the food tray. Set the timer to steam for 14-16 minutes, until the spinach is just tender.

While the spinach is steaming, in a small non-reactive bowl whisk together the tangerine juice, sherry, zest, shallot and salt. Slowly whisk in the olive oil until an emulsion forms.

To serve, place the steamed spinach in a shallow bowl. Sprinkle the cranberries over the top of the spinach and gently toss with the *Tangerine Vinaigrette*. Serve immediately.

Serves 3-4.

Calories 169 Total Fat 14 g. Saturated Fat 2 g. % Calories from Fat 75
Carbohydrates 7 g. Protein 3 g. Cholesterol 0 mg. Sodium 90 mg.

Mini Pumpkins with Swiss Cheese

A great vegetable dish for the harvest days of the year.

8 miniature	pumpkins, 1/4-inch tops cut, seeded
2 pounds	Yukon gold potatoes, peeled and cubed
1 small	butternut squash, seeded and quartered
2 tablespoons	butter or margarine
1/8 teaspoon	ground nutmeg
1/8 teaspoon	ground cloves
1/2 cup	light cream
1 cup	smoked Swiss cheese, shredded
1/2 teaspoon	salt
1/2 teaspoon	ground black pepper

Preheat the oven to 325°F. Place the prepared pumpkins on an ungreased baking sheet and bake 20 to 25 minutes until the pumpkin shells are soft.

Following the owner's manual directions, place the potatoes and squash in the food tray. Set the timer to steam for 45 minutes or until the vegetables are tender. Allow the vegetables to cool slightly. Carefully remove the steamed pulp from the squash shell and place the pulp back into the food tray with the potatoes. Attach the mixing arm and mix until the vegetables are blended. Add the butter, nutmeg, cloves, cream, Swiss cheese, salt and pepper and mix until the vegetables are fluffy.

Spoon the vegetables into the softened pumpkin shells, and place any remaining vegetables in a casserole dish and cover. Place the stuffed pumpkins into a 15 x 10-inch baking pan. Cover the pan loosely with foil and bake for 15 to 20 minutes or until thoroughly heated.

Makes 8 servings.

Calories 187   Total Fat 10 g.   Saturated Fat 6 g.   % Calories from Fat 46
Carbohydrates 18 g.   Protein 8 g.   Cholesterol 33 mg.   Sodium 183 mg.

Fresh Green Bean & Red Pepper Salad

Steam the beans until tender, yet crisp. Set the timer a bit early to ensure that the beans do not overcook.

1 pound	fresh green beans, rinsed and cut in half
1 large	red bell pepper, thinly sliced
1/2 small	purple onion, thinly sliced
1½ cups	fresh raspberries, divided
3 tablespoons	raspberry vinegar
1 teaspoon	shallot, minced
1/8 teaspoon	dry mustard
1/4 teaspoon	dried oregano
	salt and pepper to taste
1/4 cup	extra virgin olive oil

Following the owner's manual instructions, place the green beans in the food tray. Set the timer to steam for 60 minutes or until the beans are just tender. Remove the beans, cool, and place them in the refrigerator to chill.

In a large salad bowl, combine the chilled green beans, red bell pepper slices, purple onion slices and 1/2 cup of the raspberries and toss gently.

In a blender, combine the remaining raspberries, raspberry vinegar, shallot, mustard, oregano and salt and pepper. While the blender is running, slowly add the olive oil until an emulsion forms. Drizzle the dressing over the vegetables and toss gently. Serve immediately.

Serves 4.

🍴

Calories 209   *Total Fat 15 g.*   *Saturated Fat 2 g.*   *% Calories from Fat 60*
Carbohydrates 19 g.   *Protein 3 g.*   *Cholesterol 0 mg.*   *Sodium 8 mg.*

Tri-Pepper Potato Salad

Yummy and sure to gather compliments from any gathering of friends and family.

2 pounds	white potatoes, peeled and cubed
1/3 cup	celery, chopped
1/3 cup	lowfat mayonnaise
1/3 cup	red onion, peeled and minced
1/2	red bell pepper, chopped
1/2	yellow bell pepper, chopped
1/2	green bell pepper, chopped
1/4 cup	lowfat milk
3 tablespoons	white vinegar
1 tablespoon	dry mustard
1 teaspoon	salt
1/2 teaspoon	ground black pepper
1 teaspoon	fresh dill, minced
1/2 teaspoon	celery seed
	ground paprika for garnish

Following the owner's manual directions, attach the mixing arm and place the potatoes in the food tray. Set the timer to steam and automatic mash for 35-45 minutes, or until the potatoes are tender.

When the mashing cycle ends, add the celery, mayonnaise, onion, bell peppers, milk, vinegar, mustard, salt, pepper, dill and celery seed to the potatoes. Stir with a plastic spoon just until the ingredients are mixed. Place the salad in a serving bowl, cover and refrigerate until the salad is chilled. To serve, sprinkle the paprika over the top of the salad.

Makes 4 to 6 servings.

Calories 70 Total Fat 2 g. Saturated Fat <1 g. % Calories from Fat 19
Carbohydrates 12 g. Protein 3 g. Cholesterol 1 mg. Sodium 532 mg.

Chilled Asparagus Salad with Chardonnay Dressing

An elegant salad for luncheon or a light dinner meal.

1 pound	fresh asparagus, rinsed and cut into 1-inch pieces
2 medium	firm ripe tomatoes, chopped
1/2 small	red onion, thinly sliced
1/2 cup	Kalamata Greek olives
1/2 cup	Feta cheese, cubed
2 tablespoons	balsamic vinegar
1 teaspoon	Dijon mustard
1 teaspoon	fresh basil, minced
1 tablespoon	Chardonnay wine
	salt and pepper to taste
1/4 cup	extra virgin olive oil

Following the owner's manual directions, place the asparagus in the food tray. Set the timer to steam for 30-35 minutes, or until the asparagus is just tender. Remove the asparagus, cool and then chill.

In a large salad bowl, gently combine the chilled asparagus, tomatoes, onion, olives and cheese. In a blender combine the vinegar, mustard, basil, Chardonnay and salt and pepper. With the blender still running, add the olive oil slowly until the mixture becomes emulsified. Drizzle the dressing over the salad and toss gently. Serve immediately.

Serves 4.

🍴

Calories 279 *Total Fat 24 g.* Saturated Fat 5 g. *% Calories from Fat 75*
Carbohydrates 11 g. **Protein 6 g.** Cholesterol 17 mg. **Sodium 440 mg.**

Chapter Four

Delicious Dinner Entrées

Steaming foods is a primary tradition in China and is a method of food preparation in many countries around the world. Because steaming provides a moist method of heat for cooking meats, poultry and fish that tenderizes as foods cook, chefs like to use this method for the most delicate seafood and poultry dishes.

What can you steam for dinner tonight? Try *Scallops en Brochette with Lemon Butter*, *Prawns Primavera with Farfalle* or *Steamed Salmon Steaks with Thai Glaze*. Each entrée provides healthy seafood partnered with delicious sauces or glazes. Use *Cajun Seafood Cioppino* if you are feeding a crowd and try *Lobster Tails with Orange & Lemon Glaze* for a special occasion.

In addition to using each of the recipes in this chapter, look for ways to adapt your own recipes to steam instead of frying or sautéing. Steam boneless chicken to add to salads, soups and stews. Steam delicate seafood and fish to retain the best flavors of each. Try Chinese dim sum and potstickers for a fun casual dinner with friends. All of these entrées become healthful choices because fat, oil or butter can be eliminated, leading you to a better lifestyle.

Scallops en Brochette with Lemon Butter

Steam the scallops until no longer opaque and cover each with hot lemon butter.

1 pound	fresh sea scallops, rinsed
1	purple onion, cut into quarters
4-inch	bamboo skewers, water-soaked
1/4 cup	butter or margarine
1 teaspoon	grated lemon peel
1 tablespoon	fresh lemon juice
1/2 teaspoon	fresh parsley, minced
1/2 teaspoon	fresh marjoram, minced
	fresh spinach leaves for presentation

Thread the scallops and onion alternately on the bamboo skewers. Following the owner's manual directions, place the brochettes in the food tray. Set the timer to steam for 13-17 minutes or until the scallops are cooked through.

In a small saucepan melt the butter and add the lemon peel, lemon juice, parsley and marjoram and heat. Simmer for 2 minutes. To serve, place the fresh spinach leaves on the platter, place the scallop brochettes on the spinach and drizzle the hot lemon butter over all. Serve immediately.

Serves 2-3.

Calories 294   Total Fat 17 g.   Saturated Fat 10 g.   % Calories from Fat 53
Carbohydrates 9 g.   Protein 26 g.   Cholesterol 94 mg.   Sodium 253 mg.

Cajun Seafood Cioppino

A classic cioppino with an added kick of chili and cayenne!

1 pound	fresh clams, cleaned
1/2 pound	white fish, cut into 2-inch pieces (bass, cod, halibut, etc.)
1 pound	fresh shrimp, shelled and deveined
1/2 pound	fresh mussels, cleaned and de-bearded
1/2 pound	fresh crabmeat, cleaned
3 tablespoons	extra virgin olive oil
1 small	white onion, peeled and chopped
2 cloves	garlic, minced
1	green bell pepper, chopped
1/4 cup	fresh parsley, chopped
28 ounce	can crushed tomatoes
8 ounce	can tomato sauce
10 ounce	can clam juice
1 teaspoon	chili seasoning
1/2 teaspoon	cayenne pepper
1 teaspoon	black pepper
1 teaspoon	salt

Following the owner's manual instructions, place the clams and fish pieces in the food tray. Set the timer to 10 minutes. When the cycle stops, add the shrimp and mussels. Set the timer for 10-15 minutes. Check the seafood. When done, the clams and mussels will open and the shrimp will be pink.

In a large stockpot, heat the oil on medium-high heat. Add the onion and garlic and sauté until the onions are translucent, stirring occasionally. Add the remaining ingredients and heat and stir until the sauce is simmering, about 3 minutes.

Add the seafood and shellfish, including the crabmeat, to the sauce, using a large slotted spoon and simmer for 3 minutes. Adjust seasonings, if needed.

Serves 6-8.

Calories 276 Total Fat 10 g. Saturated Fat 1 g. % Calories from Fat 31
Carbohydrates 13 g. Protein 34 g. Cholesterol 130 mg. Sodium 962 mg.

Prawns Primavera with Farfalle

A beautiful presentation at the table with the colorful vegetables, prawns and farfalle pasta.

1 cup each	onion, bell peppers, carrots, broccoli and celery, julienned
1½ pounds	fresh prawns, shells removed, deveined
1 cup	light cream
1/2 cup	freshly grated lowfat Parmesan cheese
1 tablespoon	fresh basil, chopped
	salt and pepper to taste
8 ounces	cooked farfalle pasta, drained
	basil leaves for garnish

Following the owner's manual directions, place the prepared vegetables in the food tray. Place the fresh prawns on top of the vegetables. Set the timer to steam for 15-18 minutes or until the prawns are cooked through and the vegetables are tender-crisp.

In a saucepan over medium heat, combine the cream, Parmesan cheese, basil and the salt and pepper. Bring to a low simmer.

To serve, place the farfalle on a large serving platter. Cover with the prawns and vegetables and pour the primavera sauce over all. Garnish with basil leaves and serve immediately.

Serves 4.

❦❦❦

Calories 594   *Total Fat 18 g.*   Saturated Fat 8 g.   *% Calories from Fat 27*
Carbohydrates 61 g.   *Protein 47 g.*   Cholesterol 300 mg.   *Sodium 471 mg.*

Lobster Tails with Orange & Lemon Glaze

Carefully steam the lobster until it is no longer opaque and watch the lobster to ensure that it does not overcook.

2 8 ounce	**fresh or frozen lobster tails**
3 cups	**orange juice**
1 stalk	**lemongrass, crushed**
1/4 teaspoon	**ground ginger**
1/8 teaspoon	**dried chile peppers**

Thaw the lobster, if frozen. Rinse the lobster tails and pat dry with paper towels. Cut the tails by using kitchen shears or a sharp knife to cut lengthwise through the hard shells and meat. Following the owner's manual directions, place the lobster in the food tray. Set the timer to steam for 25-35 minutes, or until the lobster is cooked through.

In a saucepan over medium heat, combine the orange juice, crushed lemongrass, ground ginger and dried chile peppers. Cook and reduce until the sauce thickens.

To serve, place the steamed lobster on individual plates and drizzle the orange and lemon glaze over the lobster tails. Serve immediately.

Makes 4 servings.

Calories 187 Total Fat 2 g. Saturated Fat <1 g. % Calories from Fat 7
Carbohydrates 20 g. Protein 23 g. Cholesterol 108 mg. Sodium 338 mg.

River Trout with Smoked Almonds

*Catch some trout at your local grocery store
and enjoy this delicious entrée.*

2 8 ounce	whole river trout, rinsed and patted dry
1 tablespoon	freshly squeezed lemon juice
2 cloves	garlic, crushed
1/2 cup	smoked almonds, chopped
2 tablespoons	fresh parsley, chopped
	salt and pepper to taste
3 tablespoons	butter or margarine

Sprinkle the trout with the lemon juice. Divide the garlic, almonds and parsley evenly and place half inside each trout. Sprinkle salt and pepper over each. Following the owner's manual directions, place the trout in the food tray. Set the timer to steam for 25-30 minutes, or until the fish flakes easily and is cooked through. Garnish with additional parsley, if desired.

Serves 2.

🍴

Calories 642   Total Fat 45 g.   Saturated Fat 16 g.   % Calories from Fat 63
Carbohydrates 6 g.   Protein 53 g.   Cholesterol 183 mg.   Sodium 252 mg.

Steamed Salmon Steaks with Thai Glaze

A sweet and tangy sauce covers rich salmon steaks.

2	salmon steaks, 1-inch thick
2 tablespoons	soy sauce
1 teaspoon	white vinegar
2 tablespoons	honey
1/2 teaspoon	Asian chili oil
2 stalks	Asian lemon grass, rinsed

Following the owner's manual instructions, place the salmon steaks in the food tray. Set the timer to 15-20 minutes and steam until the salmon flakes and is no longer moist inside.

In a small saucepan, whisk together the soy sauce, vinegar, honey and chili oil. Simmer, stirring occasionally, for 5 minutes until the sauce is reduced and thickened.

To serve, plate the steaks and spoon the glaze over each steak. Garnish with the lemon grass.

Serves 2.

♨️🍴

Calories 289   Total Fat 13 g.   Saturated Fat 3 g.   % Calories from Fat 41
Carbohydrates 17 g.   Protein 25 g.   Cholesterol 75 mg.   Sodium 974 mg.

Shredded Chicken &
Caramelized Maui Onion Tartlette

*Maui onions are small and sweet and they are good companions
to chicken and cheese in this tartlette.*

2 large	boneless, skinless chicken breasts
3	sweet Maui onions, peeled and cut into ¼-inch slices
1 teaspoon	extra virgin olive oil
2 cups	egg substitute
1/4 cup	green bell pepper, chopped
1/2 teaspoon	black pepper
1/2 teaspoon	salt
1/2 cup	Swiss cheese, shredded

Following the owner's manual instructions, place the chicken breasts in the food tray. Set the timer to 35-40 minutes. When the steaming cycle stops, check the chicken. It should be white with no pink remaining. If not, continue steaming for 5 minutes. Cool the chicken and shred into small pieces.

While the chicken steams, prepare the onions. In a large skillet, heat the oil over medium-high heat and add the sliced onions. Stir the onions and sauté until the onions are browned and the sweetness is released, about 5 to 7 minutes. Set aside.

Preheat the oven to 350°F. Lightly coat a 10-inch round ovenproof baking dish or tart pan with cooking spray. Place the onion slices in the bottom of the baking dish. Pour the egg substitute over the onion slices and add the chicken and green pepper. Sprinkle the pepper and salt over the tartlette and cover with the cheese.

Bake the tartlette for 40 minutes, or until the center is slightly firm. Cool and slice into wedges to serve.

Serves 4.

Calories 195   Total Fat 5 g.   Saturated Fat 3 g.   % Calories from Fat 26
Carbohydrates 10 g.   Protein 25 g.   Cholesterol 33 mg.   Sodium 551 mg.

Golden-Crusted Summer Squash Tourtiere

The French word "tourtiere" can be translated as "meat pie" in English.

1 pound	Yukon Gold potatoes, peeled and cubed (substitute small white potatoes, if desired)
2	yellow summer squash, peeled and sliced
2 tablespoons	butter or margarine
1/2 cup	lowfat milk
1 teaspoon	salt
½ pound	lean ground beef
½ pound	ground sausage
1/4 cup	yellow onion, chopped
14-ounce	can diced tomatoes, with liquid
1/4 cup	canned tomato paste
1/2 cup	frozen petite peas
1/2 teaspoon	ground black pepper
1/2 teaspoon	salt
1 cup	mozzarella cheese, grated
1 tablespoon	fresh Italian parsley, chopped

Following the owner's manual directions, place the potatoes and squash in the food tray and set the timer to steam for 45 minutes or until the vegetables are tender. Attach the mixing arm, add the butter, milk and salt and mix for 10 to 20 seconds until well blended. Set the mashed vegetables aside.

Preheat the oven to 375°F. In a large skillet over medium high-heat, brown the ground beef, sausage, and onion until the meat is no longer pink and the onion is tender. Discard any grease. Stir in the undrained tomatoes, tomato paste, frozen peas and black pepper. Bring to a simmer. Transfer the meat filling to an ovenproof 2-quart dish.

Spoon the mashed vegetables over the top of the meat filling, covering the filling completely. Smooth with a spatula. Sprinkle the top with the mozzarella cheese. Bake for 30 minutes, or until the crust is golden brown. Remove the dish from the oven and let stand for 5 minutes before serving. Garnish with the fresh Italian parsley.

Makes 6 servings.

🍴

Calories 435   Total Fat 30 g.   Saturated Fat 9 g.   % Calories from Fat 60
Carbohydrates 17 g.   Protein 29 g.   Cholesterol 90 mg.   Sodium 1319 mg.

Garlic Chicken with Whipped Potatoes & Roasted Onions

Rutabagas aren't as well known as potatoes,
but they are good for you and good-tasting, too.

Whipped Rutabagas and Potatoes:

1/2 pound	russet potatoes, peeled and cubed
1/2 pound	rutabagas, peeled and cubed
3 cloves	garlic, peeled
3 tablespoons	butter or margarine
1 cup	heavy cream
1/4 teaspoon	salt
1/8 teaspoon	ground black pepper

Garlic Butter:

2 tablespoons	butter or margarine, softened
1 tablespoon	fresh snipped parsley
1½ teaspoons	garlic, minced
1 teaspoon	lemon zest
1/4 teaspoon	salt
1/4 teaspoon	ground black pepper
1 tablespoon	extra virgin olive oil
2 large	white onions, thinly sliced
4	boneless chicken breast halves

Following the owner's manual directions, steam the potatoes, rutabagas and garlic in the food tray for 45 minutes, or until the vegetables are tender. In a small saucepan, melt the butter. Stir in the cream, salt and pepper. Attach the mixing arm, drizzle the cream over the steamed vegetables and use the mix button to pulse for 10 to 20 seconds until well blended.

To make the *Garlic Butter*, combine the butter, parsley, garlic, lemon zest, salt and black pepper in a small bowl. Set aside.

Preheat the oven to 425°F. Brush the olive oil on a jellyroll pan. Place the onions in a single layer in the pan. Gently separate the skin from each chicken breast and spread 1/4 of the *Garlic Butter* between the skin and the meat. Place each stuffed chicken breast on top of the layered onions. Bake in the oven for 30 to 35 minutes, or until the chicken is completely cooked and no pink remains.

To serve, place a large spoonful of *Whipped Rutabagas and Potatoes* on 4 individual plates. Cover the vegetables with the roasted onions and place a chicken breast on top.

Makes 4 servings.

†|†

Calories 517 **Total Fat 42 g.** *Saturated Fat 24 g.* *% Calories from Fat 71*
Carbohydrates 17 g. **Protein 20 g.** *Cholesterol 164 mg.* **Sodium 386 mg.**

Green Chile-Stuffed Tacos

Nothing ordinary about these tacos!

1 pound	russet potatoes, peeled and cubed
2 cloves	garlic, peeled
1 pound	ground beef
1 ounce	pkg. taco seasoning
2 tablespoons	butter
1/4 cup	lowfat milk
1 4-ounce	can diced green chiles
12	soft corn tortillas
1 cup	Mexican cheese, shredded (substitute cheddar, if desired)
1 small	yellow onion, diced
2 cups	iceberg lettuce, shredded
1	large, ripe tomato, sliced
	sour cream and salsa for garnish

Following the owner's manual directions, attach the mixing arm and place the potatoes and the garlic in the food tray. Set the timer to steam and automatic mash for 35-40 minutes, or until the potatoes are tender.

In a skillet over medium-high heat, brown the hamburger. Discard any excess grease. Add the package of taco seasoning and stir to combine. Reduce the heat to warm and cover.

When the mashing cycle ends, add the butter and milk and use the mix button to pulse for 10 to 20 seconds. Add the chiles and mix for 10 seconds until blended.

To serve, spread the spicy mashed potatoes on each tortilla. Spoon the hamburger into the tortillas and top each with the cheese, onion, lettuce and tomato. Offer the sour cream and salsa as a garnish.

Makes 6 servings.

🍴

Calories 459   *Total Fat 25 g.*   Saturated Fat 12 g.   *% Calories from Fat 48*
Carbohydrates 37 g.   **Protein 24 g.**   Cholesterol 81 mg.   **Sodium 771 mg.**

Asian Plum Chicken

A beautiful plum sauce is created for this easy main dish.
Try serving with a fresh fruit salad and couscous.

2 pounds	**chicken pieces**
1/2 cup	**plum preserves**
1 tablespoon	**soy sauce**
1 teaspoon	**hoisin sauce**
1/4 cup	**orange juice**
1 teaspoon	**cornstarch**

Following the owner's manual instructions, place the chicken in the food tray. Set the timer to 35-45 minutes. Check the chicken. The chicken should be white with no pink remaining. If the chicken is not completely steamed, set the timer for 5-10 minutes and continue steaming.

Ten minutes before the chicken is done, prepare the plum sauce by combining the preserves, soy sauce, and hoisin sauce in a small saucepan. Cook and stir on medium heat just until the sauce boils. In a small cup, whisk together the orange juice and cornstarch and pour into the sauce. Stir as the sauce thickens and reduce the heat to low.

Place the steamed chicken on a large platter and spoon the warm plum sauce evenly over each piece.

Serves 4.

🍴

Calories 545   Total Fat 25 g.   Saturated Fat 7 g.   % Calories from Fat 44
Carbohydrates 27 g.   Protein 47 g.   Cholesterol 152 mg.   Sodium 400 mg.

Chapter Five

Mashed Potatoes & Accompaniments

I f you are like millions of people worldwide, you find a childlike pleasure in the satisfying taste of mashed potatoes. In fact, you may have purchased your Steam 'n Mash™ specifically to prepare mashed potatoes! If so, you've made an excellent choice. You will find that mashing potatoes in the Steam 'n Mash™ is easy and the results are consistently delectable every time. Whether you use Idaho russets, Yukon Golds, red new potatoes, exotic blues or thin-skinned white potatoes, you will delight each diner with the results.

This chapter offers easy to prepare mashed potato recipes as well as elegant, company-worthy mashed potato recipes. Check out *Never-Fail Mashed Potatoes* and *Pesto Mashed Red Potatoes* for busy weeknights. Discover unique and delicious mashed potatoes in *Toasted Walnut & Pecan Potatoes*, *Onion & Dill Yellow Finn Potatoes* and a rich and sweet *Praline Sweet Potato Bake*. Whatever your choice, mashed potatoes are always a welcome addition to your meal.

Foods that contain potatoes or squash, such as *Homestyle Potato Bread* or *Garlic & Herb Foccacia Bread* are great accompaniments to your meals. The breads and biscuits in this chapter highlight the use of your Steam 'n Mash™ and make good use of a wide variety of vegetables in baked and prepared foods. Try these recipes and add creations of your own—they will all receive applause!

Never-Fail Mashed Potatoes

Simple to prepare—use this recipe for any day of the week.

2 pounds	**russet potatoes**
½-1 cup	**lowfat milk**
2 tablespoons	**margarine**
1 teaspoon	**salt**
1 teaspoon	**freshly ground black pepper**

Following the owner's manual directions, attach the mixing arm and place the potatoes in the food tray. Set the timer to steam and automatic mash for 35-45 minutes, or until the potatoes are tender.

When the mashing cycle ends, add one-fourth of the milk, margarine, salt and pepper to the potatoes. Use the mix button to blend the potatoes for 30 seconds. Add milk as needed and pulse again.

Serves 6.

*Calories 94 **Total Fat 4 g.** Saturated Fat 1 g. % Calories from Fat 41
Carbohydrates 10 g. **Protein 4 g.** Cholesterol 3 mg. Sodium 472 mg.*

Pesto Mashed Red Potatoes

Red potatoes make a pretty presentation when they are only partially peeled or not peeled at all. The pesto sauce also adds color.

2 pounds	**red potatoes, slightly peeled and quartered**
2 tablespoons	**butter or lowfat margarine**
1/4 cup	**lowfat milk**
1 teaspoon	**salt**
1 teaspoon	**ground black pepper**
1/4 cup	**prepared pesto sauce**

Following the owner's manual directions, attach the mixing arm and place the potatoes in the food tray. Set the timer to steam and automatic mash for 40-45 minutes or until the potatoes are tender.

In a small saucepan melt the butter and add the milk, salt, pepper and pesto sauce. Heat until simmering. When the mashing cycle ends, add the butter and pesto sauce to the potatoes and use the mix button to pulse the potatoes for 10 seconds. The potatoes should be lightly mashed when ready to serve.

Makes 6 servings.

Ψ¶♦

*Calories 132   **Total Fat 9 g.**   Saturated Fat 3 g.   % Calories from Fat 60*
*Carbohydrates 9 g.   **Protein 4 g.**   Cholesterol 13 mg.   **Sodium 479 mg.***

Rosemary Mashed Potatoes

Substitute fresh basil or thyme for a change of pace.

3 pounds	new potatoes, peeled and cubed
1/2 cup	lowfat margarine
2 tablespoons	fresh rosemary, minced
1 teaspoon	lemon zest, minced
1 teaspoon	salt
1/4 cup	lowfat milk

Following the owner's manual directions, attach the mixing arm and place the potatoes in the food tray. Set the timer to steam and automatic mash for 40-45 minutes or until the potatoes are tender.

In a small saucepan over medium heat, melt the margarine and add the rosemary, lemon zest, salt and milk. When the mashing cycle ends, add the sauce to the potatoes. Use the mix button to blend for 30 seconds until the potatoes are light and fluffy. Add a little milk, if needed, to thin the potatoes.

Makes 10 servings.

🍴

Calories 59   Total Fat 3 g.   Saturated Fat 1 g.   % Calories from Fat 36
Carbohydrates 7 g.   Protein 3 g.   Cholesterol <1 mg.   Sodium 333 mg.

Sweet Apple & Cranberry Mashed Potatoes

Serve with turkey, chicken or pork for an unusual twist on classic mashed potatoes.

2 pounds	russet potatoes, peeled and cubed
1 large	red apple, peeled, cored and quartered
2 tablespoons	butter or margarine
1/4 cup	apple cider
1/4 cup	low-sodium vegetable broth
1/2 teaspoon	salt
1/2 teaspoon	white pepper
1/2 teaspoon	ground allspice
1/2 cup	dried cranberries

Following the owner's manual directions, attach the mixing arm and place the potatoes and apple in the food tray. Set the timer to steam and automatic mash for 35-40 minutes or until the potatoes are tender.

In a small saucepan melt the butter and add the cider, broth, salt, pepper and allspice. Cook over low heat until warm. When the mashing cycle ends, add the sauce and cranberries to the potatoes. Use the mix button and pulse until the potatoes are fluffy.

Makes 4 servings.

Ψ¶↑

*Calories 159   Total Fat 6 g.   Saturated Fat 4 g.   % Calories from Fat 33
Carbohydrates 24 g.   Protein 5 g.   Cholesterol 17 mg.   Sodium 374 mg.*

Onion & Dill Yellow Finn Potatoes

Yellow Finn potatoes are buttery smooth—
great for mashed potatoes.

2 pounds	**yellow Finn potatoes, peeled and cubed**
1/4 cup	**butter or margarine**
1/4 cup	**sweet onion, finely chopped**
1 tablespoon	**fresh dill, chopped**
1/2 teaspoon	**salt**
1/2 teaspoon	**white pepper**
1/4 cup	**light cream**

Following the owner's manual directions, attach the mixing arm and place the potatoes in the food tray. Set the timer to steam and automatic mash for 35-40 minutes or until the potatoes are tender.

In a small saucepan melt the butter and add the onion, dill, salt, pepper and cream. Cook over low heat until warm throughout. When the mashing cycle ends, add the butter and onions to the potatoes. Use the mix button to blend the potatoes until they are light and fluffy. Serve hot.

Makes 6 servings.

Calories 132   Total Fat 10 g.   Saturated Fat 6 g.   % Calories from Fat 65
Carbohydrates 9 g.   Protein 3 g.   Cholesterol 29 mg.   Sodium 213 mg.

Garlic & Chive Yukon Gold Potatoes

Serve with any cut of beef.

2 pounds	Yukon gold potatoes, peeled and cubed
2 cloves	garlic, peeled
2 tablespoons	lowfat margarine
2 tablespoons	chives, minced
1/2 teaspoon	salt
1/4 teaspoon	ground black pepper
1/4 cup	warm lowfat milk
1/2 cup	reduced-fat cream cheese, at room temperature
	ground paprika

Following the owner's manual directions, attach the mixing arm and place the potatoes and garlic in the food tray. Set the timer to steam for 35-40 minutes or until the potatoes are tender.

When the mashing cycle ends, add the margarine, chives, salt, pepper, milk and cream cheese to the potatoes. Use the mix button to blend the potatoes until they are fluffy. Garnish the top with paprika.

Makes 4 to 6 servings.

🍴

Calories 103 Total Fat 5 g. Saturated Fat 3 g. % Calories from Fat 45 Carbohydrates 10 g. Protein 5 g. Cholesterol 15 mg. Sodium 303 mg.

Toasted Walnut & Pecan Potatoes

A little bit of preparation is required for this recipe, but the aroma of baking potatoes will bring everyone to the table.

4 large	russet potatoes, peeled and quartered
1/4 cup	walnuts, chopped and toasted
1/4 cup	pecans, chopped and toasted
1/2 cup	lowfat ricotta cheese
1 cup	lowfat sour cream
1/2 teaspoon	salt
1/4 teaspoon	ground white pepper
2 tablespoons	lowfat margarine, melted

Following the owner's manual directions, attach the mixing arm and place the potatoes in the food tray. Set the timer to steam and automatic mash for 40 minutes or until the potatoes are tender.

To toast the walnuts and pecans, place them on a baking sheet and bake in a preheated 375°F oven until they begin to brown. Watch them carefully to avoid burning. Remove from the oven to cool and reduce the oven heat to 350°F.

Lightly coat a 2-quart shallow baking dish with cooking spray. When the mashing cycle ends, add the ricotta cheese, sour cream, salt and pepper to the potatoes. Use the mix button to pulse until the potatoes are smooth.

Spoon the mashed potatoes into the prepared baking dish. Brush the top of the potatoes with the melted margarine and bake for 30 minutes. To finish, place the potatoes under the broiler and broil until the potatoes are a crispy golden brown. Sprinkle with the toasted nuts and serve.

Makes 8 servings.

🍴

Calories 156   Total Fat 8 g.   Saturated Fat 1 g.   % Calories from Fat 47
Carbohydrates 13 g.   Protein 8 g.   Cholesterol 11 mg.   Sodium 235 mg.

Creamy Dill Potato Bake

*If you are in a time crunch, omit baking the potatoes.
Simply add the cheese and bacon after mashing
and serve immediately.*

3 pounds	Yukon Gold potatoes, peeled and cubed
1 clove	garlic, peeled
1/2 cup	lowfat milk
1 cup	Neufchatel cheese
1 cup	lowfat sour cream
2 tablespoons	fresh parsley, minced
1 teaspoon	salt
1 tablespoon	fresh dill, minced
1 cup	lowfat white cheddar cheese, grated
1/2 cup	turkey bacon, cooked and crumbled

Preheat the oven to 350°F. Lightly coat a 9 x 13-inch baking pan with cooking spray.

Following the owner's manual directions, attach the mixing arm and place the potatoes and garlic in the food tray. Set the timer to steam and automatic mash for 35-40 minutes or until the potatoes are tender. When the mashing cycle ends, add the milk, cheese, sour cream, parsley, salt and dill to the potatoes. Use the mix button to pulse until the potatoes are fairly smooth.

Spoon the potatoes into the prepared baking pan. Layer the cheese and bacon over the potatoes. Cover and bake for 30 minutes or until heated through.

Makes 8 servings.

Calories 216 Total Fat 12 g. Saturated Fat 6 g. % Calories from Fat 52
Carbohydrates 13 g. Protein 13 g. Cholesterol 44 mg. Sodium 728 mg.

Dinner Thyme Potato Pancakes

A charming recipe from years gone by.

1/2 cup	dried breadcrumbs
1/2 cup	lowfat milk
1½ pounds	russet potatoes, peeled and cubed
1/4 cup	lowfat milk
1 small	white onion, finely minced
	1 egg yolk + 1 whole egg, lightly beaten
1 teaspoon	salt
1/2 teaspoon	ground black pepper
1/4 teaspoon	fresh thyme, finely minced
2 tablespoons	lowfat margarine

In a large bowl, combine the breadcrumbs and milk, cover and set aside for 1 hour.

Following the owner's manual, attach the mixing arm and place the potatoes in the food tray. Set the timer to steam and automatic mash for 35-40 minutes, or until the potatoes are tender. Add the milk and use the mix button to pulse until smooth.

In the large bowl with the soaked breadcrumbs, add the potatoes, onion, egg, salt, pepper and thyme and mix until well-blended. Heat the margarine in a large sauté pan over medium-high heat. Drop the batter by tablespoons into the pan and flatten with a spatula. Fry the pancakes until the bottom is brown and crisp. Turn the pancakes and brown the remaining side. Continue to fry the remaining batter, adding more margarine as needed. Serve the pancakes hot out of the skillet.

Makes 6 servings.

♍♉

Calories 99   Total Fat 4 g.   Saturated Fat 1 g.   % Calories from Fat 35
Carbohydrates 11 g.   Protein 5 g.   Cholesterol 73 mg.   Sodium 525 mg.

Praline Sweet Potato Bake

Good enough for Thanksgiving dinner!

3 pounds	sweet potatoes, peeled and cubed
1 tablespoon	granulated sugar
1 tablespoon	dark brown sugar
1	egg, lightly beaten
1/4 cup	lowfat milk
1/2 teaspoon	salt

Praline Topping:

1/4 cup	packed light brown sugar
1/4 cup	unsalted butter, room temperature
3/4 cup	walnuts, chopped

Preheat the oven to 350°F. Lightly coat a 9 x 13-inch baking pan with cooking spray.

Following the owner's manual directions, attach the mixing arm and place the sweet potatoes in the food tray. Set the timer to steam and automatic mash for 40-45 minutes or until the sweet potatoes are tender. When the mashing cycle ends, add the sugars, egg, milk and salt to the potatoes. Use the mix button to pulse until the potatoes are fluffy. Scoop the potatoes into the prepared pan.

In a small bowl and using a fork, blend together the brown sugar and butter. Add the walnuts and stir to combine. Sprinkle the *Praline Topping* over the potatoes and bake for 30-35 minutes.

Makes 12 servings.

🍴

Calories 234   Total Fat 9 g.   Saturated Fat 3 g.   % Calories from Fat 35
Carbohydrates 35 g.   Protein 4 g.   Cholesterol 30 mg.   Sodium 122 mg.

Sweet Potato Mousse

Whip up this recipe to accompany pork or chicken.

1 medium head	cauliflower, chopped
2 medium	sweet potatoes, peeled and cubed
1 teaspoon	caraway seeds, crushed
2 tablespoons	lowfat margarine
1/2 cup	lowfat milk, warmed
	salt and pepper to taste
	fresh parsley, minced, for garnish

Following the owner's manual directions, attach the mixing arm and place the cauliflower and sweet potatoes in the food tray. Set the timer to steam and automatic mash for 35-45 minutes or until the vegetables are tender.

Place the mashed vegetables in a large sauté pan over medium heat. Add the caraway seeds. Continue to cook and stir until the vegetables thicken. Whisk in the margarine and milk. Season with the salt and pepper.

To serve, spoon the vegetable mousse into six individual bowls and sprinkle with the fresh parsley.

Makes 6 servings.

᎗|

Calories 89   Total Fat 2 g.   Saturated Fat 1 g.   % Calories from Fat 17
Carbohydrates 17 g.   Protein 3 g.   Cholesterol 2 mg.   Sodium 81 mg.

Cheddar & Chive Mashed Potatoes

A rich and luscious potato bake.

2 pounds	russet potatoes, peeled and cubed
1 clove	garlic, peeled
2 tablespoons	chives, minced
1/2 cup	lowfat sour cream
1/2 cup	buttermilk
1 cup	reduced-fat butter crackers, finely crushed
1 cup	lowfat cheddar cheese, shredded

Following the owner's manual directions, attach the mixing arm and place the potatoes and garlic in the food tray. Set the timer to steam and automatic mash for 35-40 minutes or until the potatoes are tender. When the mashing cycle ends, add the chives, sour cream and buttermilk. Use the mix button to pulse until the potatoes are light and fluffy.

Place the potatoes on an ovenproof serving platter and sprinkle with the crackers and cheese. Broil for 3-4 minutes until browned. Serve while hot.

Makes 6 servings.

Calories 145 Total Fat 3 g. Saturated Fat 1 g. % Calories from Fat 20
Carbohydrates 20 g. Protein 9 g. Cholesterol 5 mg. Sodium 325 mg.

Exotic Blue Mashed Potatoes

Fun to try for a change of pace!

2 pounds	blue potatoes, peeled and cubed
1/4 cup	butter or margarine
1/4 cup	white onions, chopped
1 teaspoon	salt
1/2 cup	whole milk
1/2 cup	sour cream
1/4 teaspoon	ground black pepper

Following the owner's manual directions, attach the mixing arm and place the potatoes in the food tray. Set the timer to steam and automatic mash for 35-40 minutes or until the potatoes are tender.

When the mashing cycle ends, add the butter, onions, salt, milk, sour cream and pepper to the potatoes. Use the mix button to blend until the potatoes are fluffy.

Makes 4 to 6 servings.

🍴

Calories *166* **Total Fat *13* g.** *Saturated Fat 8 g.* *% Calories from Fat 66*
Carbohydrates 10 g. **Protein 4 g.** *Cholesterol 33 mg.* *Sodium 422 mg.*

Rosemary Ranch Mashed Potatoes

Good when partnered with meat loaf or tri-tip beef.

3 pounds	**russet potatoes, peeled and quartered**
2 cloves	**garlic, peeled**
1/2 cup	**whole milk**
1/4 cup	**prepared ranch-flavored salad dressing**
1 tablespoon	**lowfat margarine**
2 tablespoons	**fresh parsley, minced**
2 tablespoons	**fresh rosemary, minced**

Following the owner's manual directions, attach the mixing arm and place the potatoes and garlic in the food tray. Set the timer to steam and automatic mash for 40-45 minutes or until the potatoes are tender.

When the mashing cycle ends, add the milk, dressing, margarine, parsley and rosemary. Use the mix button to pulse until the potatoes are well-blended. Serve immediately.

Makes 6 servings.

❦❦❦

Calories 144   Total Fat 7 g.   Saturated Fat 2 g.   % Calories from Fat 44
Carbohydrates 15 g.   Protein 6 g.   Cholesterol 9 mg.   Sodium 151 mg.

Yukon Gold Potato Patties

A healthful, reduced-fat option for mashed potatoes.

1 pound	Yukon Gold potatoes, peeled and cubed
1/4 cup	white onion, chopped
1/4 cup	lowfat milk
2 tablespoons	lowfat margarine
1 teaspoon	salt
1/2 teaspoon	ground black pepper
1	egg, slightly beaten
1/2 cup	all-purpose flour

Following the owner's manual directions, attach the mixing arm and place the potatoes and onion in the food tray. Set the timer to steam and automatic mash for 35-40 minutes or until the potatoes are tender.

When the mashing cycle ends, add the milk, margarine, salt and pepper and use the mix button to blend until fluffy. Spoon the mashed potatoes into a bowl, cover and chill for 1-2 hours. Remove the chilled potatoes and add the beaten egg and mix well. Shape the potatoes into 6 patties and dust both sides of each pattie with the flour.

Coat a large sauté pan with cooking spray and heat over medium heat. Cook the patties 5 minutes on each side, or until they are golden brown. Serve hot.

Makes 6 servings.

Calories 77 Total Fat 1 g. Saturated Fat <1 g. % Calories from Fat 15
Carbohydrates 13 g. Protein 4 g. Cholesterol 1 mg. Sodium 444 mg.

Two Cheese Garlic & Basil Gnocchi

An Italian classic, gnocchi require a bit of preparation, but the results will be especially satisfying.

3 cups	russet potatoes, peeled and cubed
5 cloves	garlic, peeled
3 tablespoons	fresh basil, finely minced
2 tablespoons	fresh chervil, finely minced
1 cup	cottage cheese (substitute ricotta cheese, if desired)
1/2 cup	Romano cheese, grated
1/2 cup	Parmesan cheese, grated
4	egg whites
3 cups	all-purpose flour

Following the owner's manual directions, place the potatoes and garlic in the food tray and steam for 35-40 minutes or until the potatoes are tender. Attach the mixing arm and add the basil, chervil, cottage cheese, Romano cheese, Parmesan cheese, egg whites and flour to the tray. Mix until a sticky dough is formed. Place the dough in an oiled bowl, cover and refrigerate for 2-4 hours.

On a well-floured surface, divide the chilled dough into 8 pieces. Roll each piece into a 1-inch log. Cut each log into 1-inch pieces, and then roll each piece into a small ball. Place the small gnocchi in a single layer on a baking sheet.

Over medium-high heat, bring a large stockpot of water to a rapid boil. Working in batches, drop the gnocchi into the water, stirring lightly to ensure that the gnocchi do not stick together. Cook for 10-12 minutes. Remove the cooked gnocchi with a slotted spoon and place them in an oiled pasta bowl. Cover the gnocchi with marinara or Alfredo sauce.

Makes 6 to 8 servings (120 gnocchi).

🍴

Calories 305 Total Fat 8 g. Saturated Fat 2 g. % Calories from Fat 23
Carbohydrates 39 g. Protein 19 g. Cholesterol 10 mg. Sodium 478 mg.

Italian Gnocchi
with Fresh Tomato Sauce

*Use up extra summer tomatoes with the lively sauce
over fresh gnocchi.*

1 pound	russet potatoes, peeled and cubed
1 cup	all-purpose flour
1 teaspoon	salt
2 eggs	lightly beaten
1/8 teaspoon	ground nutmeg
pinch	ground black pepper

Fresh Tomato Sauce:

6 large	beefsteak tomatoes, coarsely chopped
1 medium	yellow onion, chopped
2 cloves	garlic, minced
2 tablespoons	fresh basil, chopped
1 tablespoon	fresh flat leaf parsley, chopped
1/4 teaspoon	ground black pepper

Following the owner's manual directions, attach the mixing arm and place the potatoes in the food tray. Set the timer to steam and automatic mash for 35-40 minutes or until the potatoes are tender. When the mashing cycle ends, add the flour, salt, eggs, nutmeg and pepper and mix until a sticky dough is formed. Place the dough in an oiled bowl, cover and refrigerate for 2-4 hours.

To make the *Fresh Tomato Sauce*, place the tomatoes, onion, garlic, herbs and pepper in a bowl and stir to mix well. Cover and let sit at room temperature for at least 30 minutes.

On a well-floured surface, divide the dough evenly into 8 pieces. Roll each piece into a 1-inch log. Cut each log into 1-inch pieces, and then roll each piece into a small ball. Store the gnocchi in single layer on a baking sheet.

Over medium-high heat, bring a large stockpot of water to a rapid boil. Working in batches, drop the gnocchi into the water, stirring lightly to ensure the gnocchi do not stick together. Cook for 10-12 minutes. Remove the cooked gnocchi with a slotted spoon and place in a large, oiled pasta bowl. To serve, ladle the *Fresh Tomato Sauce* over the gnocchi.

Makes 4 to 6 servings.

🍴

Calories 168 Total Fat 3 g. Saturated Fat 1 g. % Calories from Fat 13
Carbohydrates 30 g. Protein 8 g. Cholesterol 71 mg. Sodium 431 mg.

Winter Vegetable Whip

Golden colors and a slightly sweet flavor
make this pleasingly special.

2 cups	cauliflower, coarsely chopped
2	carrots, peeled and sliced
4	yellow Finn potatoes, peeled and cubed
1 cup	sweet onions, diced
1/4 cup	lowfat margarine
1/2 cup	lowfat milk
1/4 cup	turkey bacon, cooked and crumbled

Following the owner's manual directions, attach the mixing arm and place the cauliflower, carrots and potatoes in the food tray. Set the timer to steam and automatic mash for 35-40 minutes or until the vegetables are tender.

In a small sauté pan over medium heat, cook the onions in 1 tablespoon margarine until they are translucent. When the mashing cycle ends, add the onions, the remaining margarine and the milk. Mix until the vegetables are well blended. Spoon the vegetables into a serving bowl and sprinkle with bacon.

Makes 4 to 6 servings.

Calories 131 Total Fat 6 g. Saturated Fat 2 g. % Calories from Fat 38
Carbohydrates 14 g. Protein 7 g. Cholesterol 15 mg. Sodium 368 mg.

Veggie-Stuffed Pocket Pies

Juicy pocket pies packed with fresh vegetable goodness.

1 head	broccoli florets, chopped
1 clove	garlic, peeled and minced
1	red bell pepper, chopped
1 cup	mozzarella cheese
1/2 cup	Parmesan cheese, freshly grated
1 tablespoon	fresh oregano, minced
1 teaspoon	salt
1/2 teaspoon	ground black pepper
1 pound loaf	frozen bread dough, thawed

Following the owner's manual directions, place the broccoli, garlic and bell pepper in the food tray and set the timer to steam for 35 minutes, or until the vegetables are tender. Remove the vegetables to cool.

Preheat the oven to 375°F. In a medium bowl, combine the cooled vegetables, mozzarella cheese, Parmesan cheese, oregano, salt and pepper and mix well. On a lightly floured surface, divide the dough into 8 pieces. Roll out each piece to form a 6-inch circle. Spoon an equal amount of the vegetable and cheese filling in the center of each circle. Fold the dough over the filling to form a half-circle. Press the edges of the dough together with a fork to seal. Make a few holes in the top of each pocket with fork to allow the steam to vent.

Place the pockets on a baking sheet that has been coated with cooking spray and bake until light golden brown, about 25 minutes. Serve hot.

Makes 8 servings.

🍴

Calories 265   Total Fat 8 g.   Saturated Fat 3 g.   % Calories from Fat 25
Carbohydrates 35 g.   Protein 17 g.   Cholesterol 19 mg.   Sodium 859 mg.

Golden Potato Turnovers

*Similar to Polish halushki or palushki, polish dumplings, these
turnovers complete a holiday or special occasion.*

1 pound	Yukon Gold potatoes, peeled and quartered

Dough:

3 cups	all-purpose flour
1 teaspoon	baking powder
1/2 teaspoon	salt
2/3 cup	vegetable oil
2	eggs
2 tablespoons	water

Potato Filling:

1 cup	yellow onion, chopped
2 tablespoons	butter
1	egg
2 tablespoons	light cream
1/2 teaspoon	salt
1/4 teaspoon	ground black pepper

Following the owner's manual directions, attach the mixing arm and place the potatoes in the food tray. Set the timer to steam and automatic mash for 35-40 minutes or until the potatoes are tender.

In a large mixing bowl, combine the flour, baking powder and salt. Blend well. Create a well in the center of the flour mixture. Add the oil, eggs and water and gradually mix together, making a soft pliable dough. Knead until smooth. Cover and set aside to rest.

In a small sauté pan over medium heat, sauté the onions in the butter until the onions are golden. Remove from the heat and cool. Add the egg, cream, salt and pepper to the cooled onions and mix well. Stir the onion mixture into the mashed potatoes and mix until well-blended. Cover and set aside.

Preheat the oven to 350°F. Place the dough on a lightly floured surface and roll out to 1/8-inch thick. Using a 3-inch circular cutter, cut the dough into rounds. Place 1 tablespoon of the potato mixture in the center of the dough round. Moisten the edges of the circle a bit and pinch to seal. Place the turnovers on a baking sheet and bake for 25 to 30 minutes. Remove the turnovers to a wire rack to cool.

Makes 30 turnovers, 1 per serving.

🍴

Calories 110   Total Fat 7 g.   Saturated Fat 1 g.   % Calories from Fat 53
Carbohydrates 11 g.   Protein 2 g.   Cholesterol 24 mg.   Sodium 100 mg.

Homestyle Potato Bread

Lovely potato flavor in a sturdy bread.
Great when sliced for toast.

1 pound	russet potatoes, peeled and cubed
2 ¼ ounce	pkgs. active dry yeast
6 ½ cups	all-purpose flour
3 tablespoons	sugar
2 tablespoons	butter
2 teaspoons	salt

Following the owner's manual directions, attach the mixing arm and place the potatoes in the food tray. Set the timer to steam and automatic mash for 35-40 minutes or until the potatoes are tender. When the mashing cycle ends, cool the potatoes to 110°F.

In a large mixing bowl, combine the yeast and 1/2 cup water. Add the cooled potatoes, 2 cups of the flour, sugar, butter and salt. Beat in the remaining flour by hand, until fully incorporated. Place the dough on a lightly floured surface and knead until moderately stiff. Add more flour to the surface, if necessary. Knead for 6 to 8 minutes until the dough is smooth and elastic. Place the dough in a lightly oiled bowl and roll once to coat the top of the dough. Cover and let the dough rise in a warm place until it doubles in bulk.

Turn the dough out on a lightly floured surface. Press the dough down and knead once. Divide the dough in half and let it rise for 10 minutes. Place each half into an 8 x 4 x 2-inch loaf pan that has been coated with cooking spray and shape. Cover and let the bread stand for 35 minutes or until it has doubled. Preheat the oven to 375°F. Bake the loaves for 40 to 45 minutes. Cover the loaves with foil for the last 15 minutes of baking to prevent overbrowning. Remove the baked breads from the pans and place them on a wire rack to cool.

Makes 2 loaves; 18 servings.

∞∎∞

Calories 194   Total Fat 2 g.   Saturated Fat 1 g.   % Calories from Fat 9
Carbohydrates 38 g.   Protein 5 g.   Cholesterol 4 mg.   Sodium 262 mg.

Southern Sweet Potato Biscuits

Fresh from the South and great on Saturday mornings.

1 large	sweet potato, peeled and quartered
1/2 cup	lowfat margarine, melted
1/2 cup	lowfat milk
2 tablespoons	sugar substitute
1/4 cup	liquid egg substitute
1¼ cups	cake flour
1¼ cups	all-purpose flour
2 teaspoons	baking powder
1 teaspoon	salt

Following the owner's manual directions, attach the mixing arm and place the sweet potato in the food tray. Set the timer to steam and automatic mash for 35-40 minutes or until the potato is tender. When the mashing cycle ends, add the margarine and use the mix button to pulse for 30 seconds. Place the potato in a medium-sized bowl.

Preheat the oven to 425°F. Add the milk, sugar substitute and egg to the potato and mix. In a separate bowl, sift together the flours, baking powder and salt. Stir the dry ingredients into the potato mixture a spoonful at a time. Knead briefly in the bowl to form a soft dough. On a lightly floured surface, roll out the dough to 3/4-inch thick. Using a 2½-inch round cookie cutter, cut out the biscuits. Transfer the biscuits to an ungreased baking sheet and bake for 15 to 20 minutes, or until the tops are golden brown.

Makes 12 biscuits.

🍴

Calories 135   Total Fat 2 g.   Saturated Fat 1 g.   % Calories from Fat 15
Carbohydrates 29 g.   Protein 4 g.   Cholesterol 1 mg.   Sodium 35 mg.

Sweet Raisin Bread

A golden, raisin-studded loaf.

1 pound	sweet potatoes, peeled and quartered
2 ¼-ounce	pkgs. dry yeast
1/4 cup	warm water
1¼ cups	lowfat milk
1/4 cup	sugar substitute
1 teaspoon	salt
1/2 cup	lowfat margarine
1 cup	raisins
4½ cups	all-purpose flour
1 cup	uncooked oats
1½ teaspoon	ground cinnamon
1/4 teaspoon	ground allspice
1/3 teaspoon	ground nutmeg
1 egg	beaten with 2 tablespoons milk for glaze

Following the owner's manual directions, attach the mixing arm and place the sweet potatoes in the food tray. Set the timer to steam and automatic mash for 35-45 minutes or until the sweet potatoes are tender. When the mashing cycle ends, transfer the mashed potatoes to a bowl and refrigerate until chilled.

In a small bowl, dissolve the dry yeast in the warm water. In a small saucepan over low heat, warm the milk with the sugar substitute and salt, stirring until dissolved. Remove the milk from heat and cool to room temperature. In a large mixing bowl, cream the margarine and add the chilled sweet potatoes and raisins. Blend well. In a separate bowl stir together the flour, oats, cinnamon, allspice and nutmeg. Add the dry ingredients alternately with the dissolved yeast to the creamed mixture and blend completely. Transfer the dough to a lightly floured surface. Knead vigorously until the dough is satiny, about 10 minutes.

Place the dough in a bowl, cover and let it rise in a warm place until it has doubled in size, about 1 hour. Punch the dough down and divide into 2 equal pieces. Place each half in a loaf pan that has been coated with cooking spray and dusted with granulated sugar. Let rise for an additional hour. Bake in a preheated 400°F oven for 20 minutes. In a small bowl, combine the egg and milk to make the glaze. Brush the loaf with the glaze and continue baking for an additional 15 minutes. The loaves will bake to a golden brown.

Makes 2 loaves; 18 servings.

♨️🍴

Calories 230   Total Fat 3 g.   Saturated Fat 1 g.   % Calories from Fat 12
Carbohydrates 45 g.   Protein 7 g.   Cholesterol 13 mg.   Sodium 198 mg.

Garlic & Herb Focaccia Bread

Make these appetizers by cutting into 24 pieces.
Serve with thin-sliced Provolone or garlic-flavored
olive oil for dipping.

1 pound	russet potatoes, peeled and cubed
1/2 cup	lowfat milk
1½ teaspoons	salt, divided
1 cup	hot water, not boiling
¼-ounce	pkg. active dry yeast
1 teaspoon	sugar
4½ cups	all-purpose flour
1 tablespoon	extra virgin olive oil
	olive oil to drizzle
1 tablespoon	garlic, minced
1 tablespoon	fresh basil, minced
1 tablespoon	fresh parsley, minced

Following the owner's manual directions, attach the mixing arm and place the potatoes in the food tray. Set the timer to steam and automatic mash for 35-40 minutes or until the potatoes are tender. When the mashing cycle ends, add the milk and 1 teaspoon salt and use the mix button to pulse for 1 minute. Let stand until the potatoes cool.

In a small bowl, combine the water, yeast and sugar, stirring to combine. Let the mixture sit for 8 to 10 minutes. The yeast will begin to work and the liquid will foam. In a large bowl, combine the flour and remaining salt. Add the yeast, the cooled potatoes and the oil. Knead the dough for 5 to 8 minutes. If the dough is too sticky, add up to ½-cup additional flour, a few tablespoons at a time. Place the dough in a lightly oiled bowl and turn to coat the dough with the oil. Cover the bowl with plastic wrap and refrigerate overnight.

Spread the dough evenly onto an oiled baking sheet. Cover the dough with a damp towel and let it rise for 30 minutes. Press your fingers gently into the top of dough evenly, dimpling the surface. Cover the dough again, and let it rise until doubled in size, 1½ to 2 hours.

Preheat the oven to 425°F. Drizzle olive oil over the top of the dough and brush lightly with water. Sprinkle the focaccia with the garlic and fresh herbs. Bake for 25 to 30 minutes, or until the bread is golden brown. Cool on a wire rack and serve immediately.

Makes 12 servings.

♈♙♙

*Calories 201   Total Fat 2 g.   Saturated Fat <1 g.   % Calories from Fat 8
Carbohydrates 39 g.   Protein 6 g.   Cholesterol <1 mg.   Sodium 300 mg.*

Low Carb-Living Recipes

A low carbohydrate diet, which is high in protein and low in simple and complex sugars, can be a tasty and enjoyable style of eating and the recipes in this chapter have been created to add to that enjoyment. To create interest and variety, you'll find in this chapter spices, fresh herbs and distinctive flavorings that add special creativity to your meals. Look for jalapeño pepper, white cheddar cheese, fresh dill, French-fried onions, fresh basil and thyme—the delights are endless!

Sometimes people who adopt a low carbohydrate style of eating still long occasionally for mashed potatoes and other carbohydrate-filled foods. Your Steam 'n Mash™ easily takes center stage to satisfy those cravings. When you think about mashed potatoes, reach for *Sour Cream Faux "Mashed Potatoes."* Made from steamed, mashed cauliflower, butter and sour cream—your taste buds will dance when you taste these faux mashed potatoes!

When you want a creamy, rich treat, try the *Cheesy Asparagus Dip* with soy crisps or low carbohydrate tortilla chips. From appetizers to desserts, menu possibilities abound when using the Steam 'n Mash™ to prepare tempting low-carbohydrate dishes.

Chilean Pepper & Black Bean Dip

No boring flavors here! The peppers are loaded with antioxidants and delicious when paired with the beans.

15-ounce	can black beans, rinsed and drained
1/4 cup	red sweet pepper, seeded and chopped
1/4 cup	green sweet pepper, seeded and chopped
1/4 cup	yellow sweet pepper, seeded and chopped
1/4 cup	orange sweet pepper, seeded and chopped
1 small	red onion, chopped
1	jalapeño pepper, seeded and minced
1 tablespoon	lemon juice
1 tablespoon	lime juice
1 tablespoon	extra virgin olive oil
1 large	clove garlic, minced
	salt and pepper to taste

Following the owner's manual directions, place the beans in the food tray and set the timer to steam for 10 minutes. Attach the mixing arm and add the peppers, onion and jalapeño. Use the mix button to pulse until the ingredients are blended and slightly mashed. In a separate bowl, combine the lemon and lime juices, oil, garlic and salt and pepper. Whisk well. Pour the oil dressing over the beans and mix to blend. Spoon the dip into a serving bowl, cover and refrigerate until chilled.

Makes 10 to 12 servings as a dip;
6 to 8 servings as a side dish.

Calories 48 Total Fat 1 g. Saturated Fat <1 g. % Calories from Fat 28
Carbohydrates 6 g. Protein 2 g. Cholesterol 0 mg. Sodium 133 mg.

Cheesy Asparagus Dip

A traditional dip that is surprisingly good-for-you on a low carbohydrate diet.

2 pounds	**asparagus, trimmed and cut into 2-inch pieces**
1/4 cup	**cream cheese, softened**
1 tablespoon	**sour cream**
1/2 cup	**Parmesan cheese, finely grated**
	salt and pepper to taste

Preheat the oven to 350°F.

Following the owner's manual directions, attach the mixing arm and place the asparagus in the food tray. Set the timer to steam and automatic mash for 30-35 minutes, or until the asparagus is tender. When the mashing cycle ends, add the cream cheese, sour cream, Parmesan cheese and salt and pepper to taste. Use the mix button to pulse for 1 minute. Spoon the dip into a 9-inch square glass baking pan and bake until heated through, about 20 minutes. To serve, sprinkle grated Parmesan over the top of the dip.

Makes about 2½ cups, enough for 12 servings.

🍴

Calories 52 **Total Fat 3 g.** *Saturated Fat 2 g.* *% Calories from Fat 49*
Carbohydrates 4 g. **Protein 3 g.** *Cholesterol 9 mg.* *Sodium 79 mg.*

Spinach & Artichoke Dip

Substitute swiss chard or other leafy greens
for a change of pace.

1 cup	artichoke hearts, drained and chopped
1 cup	spinach leaves, rinsed and dried
1 clove	garlic, peeled
1/2 cup	sour cream
1/2 cup	cream cheese
1/2 cup	Parmesan cheese, grated
1 teaspoon	red pepper flakes
1/4 teaspoon	salt
1/8 teaspoon	ground black pepper

Following the owner's manual directions, attach the mixing arm and place the artichoke hearts, spinach and garlic in the food tray. Set the timer to steam and automatic mash for 14-16 minutes, or until the spinach is tender. When the mashing cycle ends, add the sour cream, cream cheese, Parmesan cheese, red pepper, salt and pepper. Use the mix button to pulse until well blended. Spoon the dip into a bowl and serve immediately, or cover and chill.

Serves 12.

🍴

Calories 115 Total Fat 10 g. Saturated Fat 5 g. % Calories from Fat 80
Carbohydrates 3 g. Protein 3 g. Cholesterol 18 mg. Sodium 234 mg.

Vegetable & Two-Cheese Dip

*Everyone will enjoy the color and appeal
of this fresh vegetable dip.*

1 medium	yellow squash, chunked
1 medium	zucchini squash, chunked
1 medium	yellow onion, peeled and quartered
1 clove	garlic, peeled
2 tablespoons	butter
1 .25 ounce	envelope unflavored gelatin
1/4 cup	cold water
1 cup	lowfat milk, heated to boiling
1 cup	sour cream
1/4 cup	Parmesan cheese, grated
1/4 cup	white cheddar cheese, grated
1 tablespoon	fresh dill, minced
1 teaspoon	salt
1/4 teaspoon	red pepper

Following the owner's manual directions, attach the mixing arm and place the zucchini and yellow squash, onion and garlic into the food tray. Set the timer to steam and automatic mash for 15-20 minutes, or until the squash are tender. When the mashing cycle ends, add the butter and use the mix button to pulse until well blended. Set aside to cool.

Using a blender, pour the water into the jar and sprinkle with the gelatin. Let stand for 2 minutes to allow the gelatin to soften. Add the hot milk and blend on low until the gelatin is completely dissolved. Add the sour cream, both cheeses, dill, salt, pepper and the cooled squash. Blend on high until smooth, about 1 minute. Spoon the dip into a bowl, cover and refrigerate until chilled. Serve with fresh vegetables.

Serves 12.

🍴

Calories 99   Total Fat 8 g.   Saturated Fat 5 g.   % Calories from Fat 70
Carbohydrates 4 g.   Protein 4 g.   Cholesterol 20 mg.   Sodium 271 mg.

Fiesta Guacamole with Tortilla Chips

Perfect snackin' food!

2 15 ounce	cans black soybeans
1 cup	sour cream
1	avocado, peeled and pitted
2 tablespoons	prepared salsa
1/2 cup	cheddar cheese, shredded
1/2 cup	black olives, sliced
15 ounces	low-carb tortilla chips, warmed

Following the owner's manual directions, attach the mixing arm and place the black soy beans in the food tray. Set the timer to steam and automatic mash for 20 minutes, or until the beans are tender. When the mashing cycle ends, add the sour cream, avocado, salsa and cheese. Use the mix button to pulse until the dip is smooth. Transfer the dip to a glass serving dish and top with a sprinkle of cheese and the black olives. Serve with the warm low carb tortilla chips.

Serves 15.

🍴

Calories 283   Total Fat 17 g.   Saturated Fat 5 g.   % Calories from Fat 56
Carbohydrates 14 g.   Protein 19 g.   Cholesterol 11 mg.   Sodium 306 mg.

Baby Zucchini & Onion Sauté

Choose very small, ripe zucchini for best results.

1 pound	baby zucchini, peeled and coarsely chopped
1 tablespoon	extra virgin olive oil
1/2 small	white onion, sliced
1/2 small	red onion, sliced
3 tablespoons	pecans, chopped
1 teaspoon	fresh oregano, minced
1/4 teaspoon	salt
1/8 teaspoon	ground black pepper

Following the owner's manual directions, place the zucchini into the food tray. Set the timer to steam for 15 minutes, or until the squash is just tender. In a small sauté pan over medium heat, cook the onions in the oil until tender. Add the pecans, oregano, salt and pepper and stir until warm. Add the zucchini to the pecans and onions and mix until blended. Serve immediately.

Makes 4 to 6 servings.

🍴

Calories 69 Total Fat 5 g. Saturated Fat <1 g. % Calories from Fat 64
Carbohydrates 4 g. Protein 3 g. Cholesterol 0 mg. Sodium 100 mg.

Fresh Green Bean & Sour Cream Bake

Reminiscent of the classic green bean casserole, this low carbohydrate version satisfies the palate with excellent flavor.

3 cups	fresh green beans, cleaned and ends removed
1 medium	head cauliflower, chopped
10 ½-ounce	can cream of celery soup
1 cup	sour cream
1 cup	sharp cheddar cheese, shredded
1 teaspoon	salt
1/2 teaspoon	cayenne pepper
1 teaspoon	ground paprika
6 ounce	can French fried onions

Following the owner's manual directions, place the green beans in the food tray and set the timer to 30 minutes. When the cycle stops, add the cauliflower to the beans and set the timer to 30 minutes. Turn the vegetables into a 9 x 11-inch baking dish that has been lightly coated with cooking spray.

Preheat the oven to 350°F. Mix together in a medium-sized bowl, the soup, sour cream, cheese, salt and pepper and pour over the vegetables. Sprinkle the top with the paprika and scatter the onions over the top. Bake for 20-30 minutes, or until golden brown and bubbly.

Makes 8 servings.

╫╢●

Calories 247 Total Fat 18 g. Saturated Fat 8 g. % Calories from Fat 64
Carbohydrates 17 g. Protein 6 g. Cholesterol 23 mg. Sodium 587 mg.

Monterey Jack Cheese Stuffed Yellow Squash

Serve with barbecued poultry, pork or beef.

4 small	yellow squash, halved
2	russet potatoes, peeled and quartered
1/2	white onion, coarsely chopped
1 teaspoon	prepared mustard
2 tablespoons	whole wheat bread crumbs
1/4 cup	Monterey Jack cheese, shredded
	salt and pepper to taste

Following the owner's manual directions, place the squash, potatoes and the onion in the food tray. Set the timer to steam for 35-40 minutes, or until the potatoes and squash are tender. Place 5 squash halves on a cookie sheet and cover to keep warm. Remove the squash from the remaining shells and place it back into the food tray. Discard the empty shells. Attach the mixing arm and use the mix button to pulse until the squash, potatoes and onion are blended. Add the mustard, enough bread crumbs to bind the vegetables together, cheese and the salt and pepper. Pulse for 1 minute. Spoon the filling into the squash shells, mounding it liberally in each shell. Place the filled shells under the broiler and warm. Serve immediately.

Makes 8 servings.

♯¶♦

Calories 53   Total Fat 1 g.   Saturated Fat <1 g.   % Calories from Fat 20
Carbohydrates 8 g.   Protein 3 g.   Cholesterol 4 mg.   Sodium 42 mg.

Sour Cream Faux "Mashed Potatoes"

Begging for mashed potatoes?
Try these excellent faux potatoes instead.

1 small	head cauliflower, chopped
2 tablespoons	sour cream
1 tablespoon	butter
1 teaspoon	salt
1 teaspoon	ground black pepper
	minced chives for garnish

Following the owner's manual directions, attach the mixing arm and place the cauliflower into the food tray. Set the timer to steam and mash for 35-45 minutes, or until the cauliflower is tender. When the mashing cycle ends, add the sour cream, butter, salt and pepper and use the mix button to pulse until well blended. Serve with a sprinkle of minced chives.

Makes 4 servings.

⍦⍦

Calories 60 Total Fat 4 g. Saturated Fat 3 g. % Calories from Fat 65
Carbohydrates 4 g. Protein 1 g. Cholesterol 13 mg. Sodium 607 mg.

Hungarian Chicken Soup

This is the kind of soup that cries out for your favorite additions.
Add extra vegetables, herbs or spices as you like.

1 medium	head cauliflower, coarsely chopped
2 tablespoons	extra virgin olive oil
2 ribs	celery, sliced
1	sweet onion, minced
1 cup	carrots, peeled and sliced
6 cups	low-sodium chicken broth
1	dried bay leaf
1 teaspoon	ground paprika
1 cup	cooked chicken, shredded
1 tablespoon	fresh parsley, minced
	salt and pepper to taste

Following the owner's manual directions, attach the mixing arm and place the cauliflower into the food tray. Set the timer to steam and automatic mash for 35-45 minutes, or until the cauliflower is tender.

In a large saucepan, sauté the celery, onion and carrots in the olive oil over medium heat. Add the mashed cauliflower to the vegetables and stir. Add the chicken broth, bay leaf, paprika, chicken, parsley, salt and pepper to taste. Simmer for 15 minutes or until the soup is heated thoroughly. Remove the bay leaf and serve hot in individual bowls.

Makes 5 servings.

🍴

Calories 162   Total Fat 7 g.   Saturated Fat 1 g.   % Calories from Fat 37
Carbohydrates 12 g.   Protein 14 g.   Cholesterol 24 mg.   Sodium 361 mg.

Rich & Creamy Broccoli Soup

"Rich" is the word to describe this thick soup.
A great main course dish.

1½ cups	fresh broccoli, chopped
1/2 small	red onion, peeled and halved
1 tablespoon	butter
2½ cups	light cream
1 cup	cream cheese, softened
2 cups	cheddar cheese, shredded
	cheddar cheese for garnish

Following the owner's manual directions, attach the mixing arm and place the broccoli and onion in the food tray. Set the timer to steam and automatic mash for 30-40 minutes, or until the broccoli is tender. When the mashing cycle ends, add the butter and use the mix button to pulse until blended.

In a medium saucepan over low heat, combine the cream, cream cheese and cheddar cheese and cook until melted together. Do not bring to a boil. Add the broccoli mixture and continue cooking and stirring until the soup is heated thoroughly. To serve, ladle into individual bowls and top with cheddar cheese.

Makes 5 servings.

Ψ¦!

Calories 534   Total Fat 47 g.   Saturated Fat 31 g.   % Calories from Fat 79
Carbohydrates 10 g.   Protein 19 g.   Cholesterol 147 mg.   Sodium 499 mg.

Jarlsburg Cheese Soup

Creamy, buttery flavors abound with the addition of Jarlsburg cheese.

1 medium	head cauliflower, chopped
1/4 cup	butter
1	yellow onion, chopped
1 large	carrot, chopped
1 tablespoon	fresh basil, chopped
1 tablespoon	fresh thyme, chopped
1/4 cup	all-purpose flour
6 cups	low-sodium chicken broth
1 teaspoon	salt
1/4 teaspoon	ground white pepper
2 cups	light cream
2½ cups	Jarlsburg cheese, shredded

Following the owner's manual directions, place the cauliflower in the food tray. Set the timer to steam for 35-45 minutes, or until the cauliflower is tender. Set aside to cool.

In a large saucepan over medium heat, melt the butter. Sauté the onion and carrot for 10 minutes, stirring occasionally. Add the basil and thyme and cook for another minute. Add the flour, stir, and reduce the heat. Gradually stir in the chicken broth until it is smooth. Sprinkle in the salt and pepper and add the cooled cauliflower. Simmer uncovered for 30 minutes, stirring occasionally. If desired, you may puree the soup in a blender and return it to the saucepan. Add the cream and cheese and cook until the cheese is melted. Serve hot in individual bowls.

Makes 12 servings.

Calories 215   Total Fat 17 g.   Saturated Fat 10 g.   % Calories from Fat 68
Carbohydrates 8 g.   Protein 9 g.   Cholesterol 51 mg.   Sodium 493 mg.

Acorn Squash Soup

Vibrant yellow soup that can be served hot or chilled.

1 large	acorn squash, peeled and seeded
3 tablespoons	butter
1 small	yellow onion, chopped
6 cups	low-sodium chicken broth
1 cup	dry white wine
2 teaspoons	lemon juice
1 teaspoon	lemon zest
1/2 teaspoon	ground white pepper
1 cup	light cream

Following the owner's manual directions, attach the mixing arm and place the squash in the food tray. Set the timer to steam and automatic mash for 35-45 minutes, or until the squash is tender. Set aside to cool.

In a stockpot over medium heat, melt the butter and add the onion to sauté until tender. Add the chicken broth, wine and cooled squash. Bring the soup to a boil, reduce the heat and simmer for 10 minutes. Add the lemon juice, zest and pepper. Stir in the cream and cook over low heat until heated thoroughly. This soup may be served hot or cold

Makes 10 servings.

¶¶¶

*Calories 105   Total Fat 6 g.   Saturated Fat 4 g.   % Calories from Fat 53
Carbohydrates 7 g.   Protein 2 g.   Cholesterol 19 mg.   Sodium 155 mg.*

Apricot Dijon Chicken

Although this is a low carbohydrate dish, everyone will be tempted by these savory flavors.

2½ pounds	boneless, skinless chicken thighs
1 tablespoon	extra virgin olive oil
1 cup small	frozen onions
3 large	carrots, sliced ½ -inch thick
1 pound	new potatoes, quartered
1 teaspoon	salt
1 teaspoon	ground black pepper
1/2 cup	low-sodium chicken broth
1/3 cup	*Apricot Sauce*

In a large sauté pan over medium-high heat, brown the chicken in the olive oil and set aside. Following the owner's manual instructions, place the onions, potatoes and carrots in the food tray. Arrange the chicken thighs on top of the vegetables and sprinkle the salt and pepper over all. Set the timer to steam for 45 minutes. When the chicken is cooked through completely and no pink remains, remove the chicken and vegetables. Place on a large serving platter and cover tightly to keep warm.

Prepare the Apricot Sauce and spoon it over the chicken and vegetables just before serving.

Makes 8 servings.

🍴

Apricot Sauce:

2 cups	apricots, peeled and seeded
1/4 cup	cream cheese, softened
1/2 cup	sour cream
1 teaspoon	lemon juice
1 teapoon	sugar substitute
1 tablespoon	Dijon mustard
1/8 teaspoon	ground nutmeg

Following the owner's manual directions, attach the mixing arm and place the apricots in the food tray. Set the timer to steam and automatic mash for 15-20 minutes, or until the apricots are tender. When the mashing cycle ends, add the cream cheese, sour cream, lemon juice, sweetener, mustard and nutmeg and use the mix button to pulse for 1 minute. Spoon the apricot sauce over the chicken.

🍴

Calories 104   Total Fat 5 g.   Saturated Fat 1 g.   % Calories from Fat 40
Carbohydrates 10 g.   Protein 7 g.   Cholesterol 25 mg.   Sodium 362 mg.

Marjoram-Stuffed Chicken Breasts

Browning the chicken for a few minutes adds to the beauty of the finished dish at the table.

1½ cups	button mushrooms
1 clove	garlic, peeled
1	red pepper, seeded and halved
1	green pepper, seeded and halved
1 tablespoon	fresh marjoram, crushed
4	boneless, skinless chicken breast halves
4 slices	Swiss cheese
1 teaspoon	extra virgin olive oil

Following the owner's manual directions, place the mushrooms, garlic and peppers in the food tray. Set the timer to steam for 15 minutes or until the vegetables are tender. Attach the mixing arm and add the marjoram. Use the mix button to pulse the vegetables for 1 minute. Set aside.

Cut a horizontal slit in the thickest part of the chicken breasts, forming a pocket. Place a slice of the Swiss cheese and a spoonful of the vegetable stuffing into each pocket and secure with toothpicks. In a large sauté pan over medium-high heat, cook the chicken breasts in the oil until brown on both sides. Place the chicken in the food tray and set the timer to steam for 35 minutes. Steam until the chicken is completely cooked and no pink remains.

Makes 4 servings.

🍴

Calories 227 Total Fat 10 g. Saturated Fat 5 g. % Calories from Fat 40
Carbohydrates 8 g. Protein 26 g. Cholesterol 67 mg. Sodium 123 mg.

Cheese & Spinach-Filled Meatloaf

*Use lean ground beef or ground sirloin and handle
the meat carefully to avoid overmixing.*

1½ cups	fresh spinach, drained and roughly chopped
1½ pounds	lean ground beef
1/4 cup	Romano cheese, grated
1/4 cup	Parmesan cheese, grated
1/2 cup	Gruyere cheese, grated
2 tablespoons	prepared mustard
1 teaspoon	salt
1/2 teaspoon	ground black pepper
1 teaspoon	garlic powder
2 medium	eggs
	minced chives for garnish

Cauliflower Crust:

1/2	head cauliflower, chopped
2 tablespoons	sour cream
1 tablespoon	butter
1 teaspoon	salt
1/2 teaspoon	ground black pepper

Following the owner's manual directions, attach the mixing arm and place the spinach in the food tray. Set the timer to steam and automatic mash for 15 minutes, or until the spinach is tender.

Preheat the oven to 375°F. When the mashing cycle ends, add the beef, cheeses, mustard, salt, pepper, garlic powder and eggs to the spinach. Use the mix button to pulse until the ingredients are integrated. Do not mix for more than 1 minute. Mold the meatloaf into a 9 x 5-inch loaf pan. Bake for 50 minutes.

While the meatloaf is baking, thoroughly clean the Steam 'n Mash™. Attach the mixing arm and place the cauliflower in the food tray. Set the timer to steam and automatic mash for 35-45 minutes, or until the cauliflower is tender. When the mashing cycle ends, add the sour cream, butter, salt and pepper and use the mix button to pulse for 1 minute. Spoon the cauliflower over the top of the meatloaf, using a spatula to smooth evenly. Bake the meatloaf for an additional 10 minutes until the cauliflower is slightly browned. To serve sprinkle the meatloaf with chives and slice.

Makes 6 servings.

🍴

Calories 428 Total Fat 31 g. Saturated Fat 14 g. % Calories from Fat 65
Carbohydrates 5 g. Protein 32 g. Cholesterol 179 mg. Sodium 1169 mg.

Swiss Chicken Breasts

Swiss cheese makes these chicken breasts special!

3 small	yellow squash, chunked
1 tablespoon	butter
2 slices	low carb bread, cubed
1/3 cup	Swiss cheese, shredded
1/2 cup	yellow onion, minced
1/2 cup	celery, minced
1 tablespoon	fresh Italian parsley, minced
1 large	egg, lightly beaten
1/2 teaspoon	salt
1/4 teaspoon	ground black pepper
4	boneless, skin-on chicken breast halves

Following the owner's manual directions, attach the mixing arm and place the yellow squash in the food tray. Set the timer to steam and automatic mash for 15-20 minutes, or until the squash is tender. Set aside to cool. When the squash has cooled, add the butter, bread, cheese, onion, celery, parsley, egg, salt and pepper. Use the mix button and pulse to blend the ingredients.

Preheat the oven to 375°F. Loosen the skin on each of the chicken breasts to form a pocket. Stuff each pocket with one-fourth of the filling. Place the chicken in a single layer in a 9 x 13-inch baking dish that has been coated with cooking spray. Bake until the chicken is cooked through completely and the skin is crisp and golden, about 45 minutes.

Makes 4 servings.

❦

Calories *218* Total Fat *9 g.* Saturated Fat *4 g.* % Calories from Fat *36*
Carbohydrates *11 g.* Protein *24 g.* Cholesterol *113 mg.* Sodium *448 mg.*

Florentine Flank Steak

Carefully slice the steamed steak into ½-inch pieces for a beautifully completed entrée.

2 cups	fresh spinach, torn into large pieces
1 cup	cream cheese, softened
1 teaspoon	salt
1 teaspoon	ground black pepper
1 lb.	beef flank steak
10½ ounce	can low-sodium beef broth
1/2 cup	red wine vinegar

Following the owner's manual directions, attach the mixing arm and place the spinach in the food tray. Set the timer to steam and automatic mash for 15 minutes, or until the spinach is tender. When the mashing cycle ends, add the cream cheese, salt and pepper and use the mix button to pulse until well blended. Set aside.

Preheat the oven to 350°F. Pound the flank steak to 1/4-inch thick. Spread the spinach and cream cheese filling evenly over the steak. Roll the steak to enclose the filling and secure with toothpicks. Place the steak roll seam side down in a roasting pan. In a small bowl, combine the broth and vinegar and mix well. Pour 2/3 of the liquid over the steak roll. Roast the steak, basting occasionally, for about 45 minutes. To serve, cut the steak roll into 1-inch slices and plate. Ladle the roasting sauce over the slices of steak.

Makes 4 servings.

🍴

Calories 418 Total Fat 32 g. Saturated Fat 18 g. % Calories from Fat 70
Carbohydrates 2 g. Protein 29 g. Cholesterol 123 mg. Sodium 866 mg.

Stuffed Turkey Tenderloins

Steaming turkey produces tenderness and the addition of sweet potatoes and apples makes these tenderloins even better.

2 medium	sweet potatoes, peeled and coarsely chopped
2 large	apples, peeled, cored and halved
1/4 cup	light cream
1 teaspoon	salt
1/2 teaspoon	ground black pepper
4	turkey tenderloins
4 slices	smoked gouda cheese

Following the owner's manual directions, attach the mixing arm and place the sweet potatoes and apples into the food tray. Set the timer to steam and automatic mash for 35-45 minutes, or until the sweet potatoes are tender. When the mashing cycle ends, add the cream, salt and pepper and use the mix button to pulse until blended, but still chunky. Set aside.

Preheat the oven to 375°F. Cut each tenderloin almost in half lengthwise. Sprinkle with salt and pepper. Spread 2 tablespoons of the potato and apple filling on one side of each tenderloin and top with a slice of cheese. Close the tenderloins using toothpicks. Arrange the tenderloins on a rimmed baking sheet. Bake for 20 minutes, or until a meat thermometer reads 160°F. Slice each tenderloin into 3/4-inch slices and arrange on individual dinner plates.

Makes 8 servings.

❦

Calories 237 **Total Fat 10 g.** *Saturated Fat 2 g.* *% Calories from Fat 17*
Carbohydrates 17 g. **Protein 20 g.** *Cholesterol 62 mg.* *Sodium 505 mg.*

Layered Vegetable Lasagna

Every delightful Italian flavor is here!

1 head	cabbage, torn into single leaves
1 teaspoon	extra virgin olive oil
1 small	yellow onion, minced
2 cloves	garlic, peeled
1	red bell pepper, seeded and chopped
1 pound	lean ground beef
8 ounce	can tomato sauce
6 ounce	can tomato paste
1 tablespoon	fresh basil, minced
1 teaspoon	salt
1/2 teaspoon	ground black pepper
1 cup	mozzarella cheese, shredded
1 cup	ricotta cheese

Following the owner's manual directions, place the cabbage leaves in the food tray. Set the timer to steam for 20-30 minutes until the cabbage is just tender. Set aside. In a large pan over medium-high heat, sauté the onion, garlic and pepper in the oil until the onions are translucent. Add the ground beef and brown thoroughly. Discard any grease. Pour the tomato sauce, paste, basil, salt and pepper over the beef mixture and mix well.

Preheat the oven to 350°F. Lightly coat a 9 x 13-inch glass baking dish with cooking spray. Line the bottom of the dish with a layer of the steamed cabbage leaves. Top the cabbage with half of the meat mixture. Spread half of the ricotta cheese over the meat and sprinkle 1/3 of the mozzarella over the ricotta. Repeat these layers until the beef is gone. Sprinkle with any remaining mozzarella and bake for 20 minutes. Uncover and bake an additional 5 minutes.

Makes 12 servings.

🍴

Calories 219 *Total Fat 13 g.* Saturated Fat 4 g. % Calories from Fat 52
Carbohydrates 11 g. Protein 17 g. Cholesterol 44 mg. Sodium 427 mg.

Chapter Seven

Grand Finale Desserts & Breakfast Treats

D essert is the perfect finish to any meal and delights all who receive the special note of an effort made in the preparation. Your Steam 'n Mash™ can bring many excellent desserts to the table and the recipes in this chapter highlight the many uses of this appliance. Whether you are looking for a rich fruit-filled dessert or a unique candy based on the rich foundation of mashed potatoes, you'll be surprised by the many ways in which the Steam 'n Mash™ can be used to create delectable, unique desserts.

Desserts are often seen as having little or no nutritional value, but your Steam 'n Mash™ allows you to base cookies, cakes, pies and more on fresh fruit and vegetables prepared for optimal nutritional use. Take a look through the recipes in this chapter to find those that you and your family will enjoy. Like applesauce? Try Raisin Nut Applesauce Cookies. Enjoy tangerines, apricots and cranberries? Look no further than Tangy Fruit Compote. Searching for something "peachy?" Try Peach Nectar Cake for your next gathering. Each of these desserts creates a delicious end-of-the-meal statement and satisfies even your most demanding guests. Enjoy!

Raisin Nut Applesauce Cookies

Soft and chewy. Perfect for lunches.

3	Jonathan Gold apples, peeled, cored and halved (substitute any baking apple, if desired)
1 cup	lowfat margarine
2	eggs (use egg substitute, if desired)
1½ cups	dark brown sugar
1/4 cup	cold coffee
3½ cups	all-purpose flour
1 teaspoon	baking soda
1 teaspoon	salt
1/2 teaspoon	ground nutmeg
1½ teaspoons	ground allspice
1 cup	golden raisins
1/2 cup	walnuts, chopped

Following the owner's manual, attach the mixing arm and place the apples in the food tray. Set the timer to steam and automatic mash for 30 minutes or until the apples are tender. When the mashing cycle ends, transfer the applesauce to a small bowl and refrigerate until cool.

In a large mixing bowl, beat together the margarine and the eggs. Add the brown sugar and mix. Add the coffee and the cooled applesauce. Mix well. In a separate bowl stir together the flour, baking soda, salt, nutmeg and allspice. Beat the dry ingredients into the creamed mixture. Stir in the raisins and walnuts. Roll the dough in plastic wrap and chill for several hours.

Preheat the oven to 400°F. Lightly coat a cookie sheet with cooking spray. Drop the chilled dough by tablespoons 2-inches apart. Bake for 9-12 minutes. Remove the cookies from the oven and let them cool on the cookie sheet before transferring them to a wire rack. Store in an airtight container.

Serves 24, 2 cookies each.

🍴

Calories 182   Total Fat 4 g.   Saturated Fat 1 g.   % Calories from Fat 20
Carbohydrates 34 g.   Protein 3 g.   Cholesterol 18 mg.   Sodium 229 mg.

Brown Sugar Zucchini Pie

*An old Southern traditional pie, the brown sugar
and zucchini pair into a sweet, rich pie.*

2 medium	yellow squash, peeled and chunked
3 medium	zucchini, peeled and chunked
1/4 cup	butter, melted
1/2 cup	dark brown sugar
1 tablespoon	vanilla extract
1 tablespoon	all-purpose flour
2	egg yolks, beaten
1/2 teaspoon	salt
1	pre-baked 9-inch pie shell
	whipped cream for garnish

Following the owner's manual directions, attach the mixing arm and place the squash in the food tray. Set the timer to steam and automatic mash for 15-20 minutes or until the squash are tender.

Preheat the oven to 375°F. When the mashing cycle ends, add the butter, sugar, vanilla, flour, egg yolks and salt and use the mix button to pulse until well blended. Spoon the squash filling into the pie shell and smooth evenly. Bake for 20-25 minutes, or until the center is firm. Remove from the oven and cool slightly before serving. Garnish with whipped cream.

Makes 8 servings.

Calories 262 Total Fat 15 g. Saturated Fat 2 g. % Calories from Fat 51
Carbohydrates 28 g. Protein 4 g. Cholesterol 68 mg. Sodium 275 mg.

Fresh Apple Spiced Cake

*Use any type of good baking apple to create
this spicy apple cake.*

2 large	Golden Delicious apples, peeled, cored and halved
1/2 cup	butter or margarine, softened
2 cups	sugar
1	egg
2½ cups	all-purpose flour
1 teaspoon	ground allspice
1/4 teaspoon	ground nutmeg
1 teaspoon	ground cinnamon
1 teaspoon	salt
2 cups	dates, chopped
1 cup	pecans, chopped
	caramel syrup for garnish

Following the owner's manual directions, attach the mixing arm and place the apples in the food tray. Set the timer to steam and automatic mash for 30-40 minutes or until the apples are tender. When the mashing cycle ends, allow the applesauce to cool.

Preheat the oven to 350°F. Lightly coat a 9 x 13-inch baking pan with cooking spray. In a large mixing bowl, cream the butter, sugar and egg. Add the cooled applesauce and mix well. In a small bowl sift together the flour, allspice, nutmeg, cinnamon and salt. Gradually add the flour mixture to the applesauce and mix until well blended. Stir in the dates and pecans. Spoon the cake batter into the prepared pan and bake for 35 minutes, or until the center of the cake springs back to the touch. Remove the cake from the oven and cool on a wire rack.

To serve, cut into individual pieces and drizzle with caramel syrup.

Makes 12 servings.

🍴

Calories 472   Total Fat 16 g.   Saturated Fat <1 g.   % Calories from Fat 29
Carbohydrates 83 g.   Protein 5 g.   Cholesterol 38 mg.   Sodium 201 mg.

Tangy Fruit Compote

*Add a bit of fruit liqueur if you want to bring
added zing to this compote.*

4 cups	dried apricots, apples and cranberries
2	navel oranges, peeled and segmented
2 cups	fresh pineapple juice
½ cup	light cream

Following the owner's manual directions, place the dried fruit and orange quarters in the food tray. Set the timer to steam for 30 minutes. When the cycle is done, remove the steamed fruit and place in a large glass pitcher. Add the pineapple juice, stir and set aside for 4 hours to allow the flavors to marry.

To serve, spoon the fruit with the juice into individual cups and top with cream.

Serves 6.

Calories 149   Total Fat 4 g.   Saturated Fat 2 g.   % Calories from Fat 24
Carbohydrates 29 g.   Protein 2 g.   Cholesterol 13 mg.   Sodium 14 mg.

Raisin, Pear & Apple Squares

Back to school treats!

1 medium	red apple, peeled, cored and halved
2 medium	Bartlett pears, peeled, cored and halved
1/2 cup	lowfat margarine
1	egg (use egg substitute, if desired)
1/2 cup	dark brown sugar
1/2 cup	granulated sugar
1 teaspoon	baking soda
1/4 teaspoon	salt
1 teaspoon	ground cinnamon
2 cups	all-purpose flour
1 teaspoon	ground allspice
1/4 teaspoon	ground cloves
1 cup	raisins

Following the owner's manual directions, attach the mixing arm and place the apple and pears in the food tray. Set the timer to steam and automatic mash for 30-40 minutes or until the fruit is tender. When the mashing cycle ends, let the fruit stand to cool.

Preheat the oven to 350°F. Lightly coat a 9 x 13-inch baking pan with cooking spray. In a medium bowl, mix together the margarine, egg and sugars until light and fluffy. In a separate bowl, stir together the baking soda, salt, cinnamon, flour, allspice and cloves. Add the flour mixture to the cooled fruit and mix. Add the creamed mixture to the fruit and mix again until the batter is well-blended. Stir in the raisins. Spoon the batter into the prepared baking pan and bake for 35 minutes, or until the center is firm to the touch. Remove from the oven and cool on a wire rack. Cut into 12 squares to serve.

Makes 12 servings.

🍴

Calories 228   Total Fat 3 g.   Saturated Fat <1 g.   % Calories from Fat 11
Carbohydrates 49 g.   Protein 3 g.   Cholesterol 18 mg.   Sodium 236 mg.

Peach Nectar Cake

Peaches steam and mash beautifully, as this cake demonstrates.

3	peaches, peeled, pitted and halved
2½ cups	all-purpose flour
2 teaspoons	baking soda
1 teaspoon	salt
1/2 teaspoon	ground nutmeg
1/2 teaspoon	ground cinnamon
1/4 teaspoon	ground cloves
3/4 cup	butter or margarine
2 cups	sugar
2 large	eggs
1½ teaspoons	vanilla extract
1/2 cup	buttermilk
1/2 cup	lowfat milk
	peach slices for garnish

Peach Nectar Frosting:

1/3 cup	butter or margarine, softened
3 cups	powdered sugar
4 tablespoons	peach nectar

Following the owner's manual directions, attach the mixing arm and place the peaches in the food tray. Set the timer to steam and automatic mash for 30 minutes or until the peaches are tender. Set aside to cool.

Preheat the oven to 350°F. Lightly coat a 9 x 13-inch baking pan with cooking spray. In a medium mixing bowl, sift together the flour, baking soda, salt, nutmeg, cinnamon and cloves. Set aside. In a separate mixing bowl, beat the butter until fluffy. Add the sugar and beat again. Add the eggs, one at a time, beating well after each addition. Add the vanilla and mashed peaches to the butter and sugar mixture. Add the dry ingredients, buttermilk and milk alternately to the peach mixture, beating well after each addition. The batter should be fairly thick. Spoon the cake batter into the prepared pan and bake for 1 hour or until center is firm. Remove the cake and cool on a wire rack.

In a small mixing bowl, beat together the butter and powdered sugar. Add the peach nectar as needed to achieve the desired consistency. Spread the frosting over the cooled cake. To serve, cut individual pieces of cake and garnish with a slice of peach.

Makes 12 servings.

🍴

Calories 535   *Total Fat 19 g.*   *Saturated Fat 11 g.*   *% Calories from Fat 31*
Carbohydrates 89 g.   **Protein 5 g.**   *Cholesterol 84 mg.*   *Sodium 441 mg.*

Harvest Apple & Pumpkin Pie

An inviting addition to traditional pumpkin pie.

1 small	pumpkin, seeded and quartered
3 medium	red apples, peeled, cored and quartered
2	eggs
2	egg whites
3/4 cup	apple juice
1½ tablespoons	honey
1/2 cup	sugar
1/2 cup	raisins
1/2 teaspoon	ground cinnamon
1 teaspoon	ground allspice
1/2 teaspoon	dried thyme
1/2 teaspoon	dried marjoram
1/2 teaspoon	salt
8-inch	pie crust
	whipped cream
	thin slices of apple

Following the owner's manual directions, place the pumpkin and apples in the food tray. Set the timer to steam for 45 minutes or until the pumpkin is tender. Remove the steamed pumpkin and spoon out the pulp, placing it back into the food tray with the apple. Discard the shell. Attach the mixing arm and use the mix button to pulse the pumpkin and apple together until pureed.

Preheat the oven to 425°F. In a medium mixing bowl, combine the eggs and egg whites and beat at high speed until blended. Add the apple juice, honey, sugar, raisins, cinnamon, allspice, thyme, marjoram and salt and mix well. When the mashing cycle ends, spoon the apple juice batter into the pureed apples and pumpkin and use the mix button to pulse until the ingredients are completely blended. Pour the batter into the prepared piecrust and smooth the top. Bake for 15 minutes, reduce the heat to 350°F and bake an additional 40 minutes.

Remove the pie from the oven and cool on a wire rack. To serve, cut into individual slices and top with fresh whipped cream and a thin slice of apple.

Makes 8 servings.

Calories 292 Total Fat 9 g. Saturated Fat 2 g. % Calories from Fat 28
Carbohydrates 49 g. Protein 5 g. Cholesterol 53 mg. Sodium 303 mg.

Coco Loco Cake

*Mashed potatoes make a smooth foundation
for this rich. chocolatey cake.*

1/2 pound	russet potatoes, peeled and cubed
1/4 cup	lowfat milk
3/4 teaspoon	salt, divided
1 cup	water, lukewarm
2 cups	all-purpose flour, sifted
1 cup	unsweetened cocoa powder
2¼ teaspoons	baking powder
1/2 teaspoon	baking soda
2/3 cup	unsalted butter
2 cups	sugar
1 1/2 teaspoon	vanilla extract
4 large	eggs
	powdered sugar

Following the owner's manual directions, attach the mixing arm and place the potatoes in the food tray. Set the timer to steam and automatic mash for 45 minutes or until the potatoes are tender.

Lightly coat a 9 x 13-inch baking pan with cooking spray and dust with flour. When the mashing cycle ends, add the milk and 1/4 teaspoon salt to the potatoes and use the mix button to pulse until blended. Transfer the potatoes to a medium mixing bowl and whisk in the water to form a thin batter. Let the potatoes cool to lukewarm. In a separate bowl, sift together the flour, cocoa, baking powder, baking soda and 1/2 teaspoon salt.

Preheat the oven to 350°F. In a large bowl, use an electric mixer on low speed to combine the butter, sugar and vanilla. Increase the speed to medium and beat for 2 minutes. Add the eggs, 2 at a time, beating at low speed until blended. Slowly add the dry ingredients and combine well. Add the potato mixture in two increments and mix. The batter may be slightly lumpy. Pour the batter into the prepared pan and spread level. Bake for 27-32 minutes, turning the pan back to front halfway during the baking time. The cake is done when a toothpick inserted in the middle comes out with a few moist crumbs. Do not overbake. Place the cake on a wire rack to cool. Sift powdered sugar over the top of the cake.

Makes 12 servings.

🍴

Calories 346 Total Fat 13 g. Saturated Fat 8 g. % Calories from Fat 33
Carbohydrates 55 g. Protein 6 g. Cholesterol 99 mg. Sodium 301 mg.

Orange & Lemon Zest Pound Cake

Special occasions call for this rich, creamy pound cake.

2 medium	russet potatoes, peeled and cubed
2 tablespoons	light cream
1/4 teaspoon	salt
3 cups	sugar
2 cups	butter
3 cups	all-purpose flour
1/4 cup	sour cream
1/4 cup	fresh squeezed lemon juice
1/3 cup	fresh squeezed orange juice
1 teaspoon	baking soda
1 teaspoon	orange zest
5 large	eggs

Orange Lemon Glaze:

2 teaspoons	orange zest
2 teaspoons	lemon zest
3 tablespoons	butter, melted
4 cups	powdered sugar, sifted
1 teaspoon	orange juice
1 teaspoon	lemon juice
	lemon zest for garnish

Following the owner's manual directions, attach the mixing arm and place the potatoes in the food tray. Set the timer to steam and automatic mash for 35-40 minutes or until the potatoes are tender. When the mashing cycle ends, add the cream and salt and mix until well blended and smooth. Cool the mashed potatoes.

Preheat the oven to 350°F. Lightly coat a 10-inch tube pan with cooking spray and dust with flour. In a large mixing bowl with an electric mixer at low speed, beat the sugar and butter until fluffy. Add the flour, sour cream, cooled mashed potatoes, lemon juice, orange juice, baking soda, orange zest and eggs. Beat on low speed until the ingredients are blended, then increase to high speed and mix for 2 minutes. Spoon the batter into the prepared pan. Bake for 1½ hours, or until a cake tester comes out clean. Cool the cake in the pan on a wire rack for 15 minutes. Using a spatula, carefully remove the cake from the pan and cool completely on the rack.

In a mixing bowl, combine the orange and lemon zest with the butter and the powdered sugar. Add the orange and lemon juices and beat until smooth. Add more or less juice for the desired consistency. Drizzle the glaze over the top of the cooled cake. Sprinkle the top of the cake with fresh lemon zest.

Makes 16 servings.

🍴

Calories 622   Total Fat 29 g.   Saturated Fat 18 g.   % Calories from Fat 41
Carbohydrates 88 g.   Protein 5 g.   Cholesterol 141 mg.   Sodium 154 mg.

Orange Walnut Cookies

Serve with Chai tea!

2 pounds	sweet potatoes, peeled and cubed
1/4 cup	lowfat milk
1/2 cup	fresh squeezed orange juice
1 teaspoon	orange extract
1 tablespoon	freshly grated orange zest
1	egg, beaten
1/2 teaspoon	ground allspice
1/3 cup	walnuts, chopped

Following owner's manual directions, attach the mixing arm and place the potatoes in the food tray. Set the timer to steam and automatic mash for 35-45 minutes or until the potatoes are tender. When the mashing cycle ends, pour the milk over the mashed potatoes and use the mix button to pulse until blended. Set aside the mashed potatoes to cool.

Preheat the oven to 350°F and lightly coat a cookie sheet with cooking spray. In a small mixing bowl, combine the orange juice, extract, zest, egg, allspice and walnuts. Stir into the cooled mashed potatoes. Mix well to combine the ingredients completely. Drop the batter by spoonfuls onto the prepared cookie sheet. Bake for 8-10 minutes or until golden.

Makes 10 servings, 2 cookies each.

Calories 137 Total Fat 3 g. Saturated Fat <1 g. % Calories from Fat 21
Carbohydrates 24 g. Protein 3 g. Cholesterol 22 mg. Sodium 21 mg.

Pumpkin Nut Cookies

Look for pumpkin pie spice in your grocery store.

1 small	pumpkin, quartered
2 cups	all-purpose flour
1 teaspoon	baking powder
1 teaspoon	baking soda
1 teaspoon	pumpkin pie spice
1/2 teaspoon	salt
1/2 cup	butter, softened
1/2 cup	granulated sugar
1/2 cup	dark brown sugar
1	egg
1 1/2 teaspoon	vanilla extract
1/2 cup	raisins
1/2 cup	walnuts, chopped

Following the owner's manual directions, place the pumpkin in the food tray. Set the timer to steam for 45 minutes, or until the pumpkin is tender. Remove the pumpkin and scoop the pulp out of the shell and back into the food tray. Discard the shell. Attach the mixing arm and mash the pumpkin until it is smooth. Transfer the pumpkin pulp to a medium bowl and set aside.

In a separate bowl, combine the flour, baking powder, baking soda, pumpkin pie spice and salt and mix with a fork. In a large bowl, combine the butter, granulated sugar and brown sugar and beat with an electric mixer until light and fluffy. Add and mix together the mashed pumpkin, egg and vanilla. Stir in the flour mixture and mix until smooth. Fold in the raisins and walnuts, cover the dough and chill for 2 hours.

Preheat the oven to 375°F. Drop the chilled dough by spoonfuls on an ungreased cookie sheet. Bake for 11 minutes or until the cookies are firm. Cool on the cookie sheet for 2 minutes and then place the cookies on wire racks. Store in an airtight container.

Makes about 18 servings, 2 cookies per serving.

Calories 189   Total Fat 8 g.   Saturated Fat 4 g.   % Calories from Fat 36
Carbohydrates 28 g.   Protein 3 g.   Cholesterol 26 mg.   Sodium 167 mg.

Apple & Raisin Sandwich Cookies

Raisins and red apples are natural complements.
This recipe calls for dark brown sugar and dark corn syrup
to sweeten them even more!

2 cups	raisins, chopped
2	red apples, peeled, cored and quartered
3 cups + 1 tablespoon	all-purpose flour, divided
2 teaspoons	baking soda
1 cup	dark brown sugar
1/2 cup	butter, whipped
5 tablespoons	dark corn syrup
2 large	eggs
1 teaspoon	vanilla extract
1 cup	granulated sugar
1/2 cup	water

Following the owner's manual directions, attach the mixing arm and place the raisins and apples in the food tray. Set the timer to steam and automatic mash for 35-40 minutes, or until the fruit is tender.

Preheat oven to 350°F. In a medium bowl, mix 3 cups flour and the baking soda and set aside. In a large bowl, combine the brown sugar, whipped butter, corn syrup, eggs and vanilla and beat until light and fluffy. Gradually stir in the dry ingredients. Roll the cookie dough 1/4-inch thick on a lightly floured surface. Cut the dough into round cookies with a 1½-inch cookie cutter. Arrange the cookies 2-inches apart on a baking sheet and bake for 11 minutes. Cool completely on a wire rack.

Spoon the mashed apples and raisins into a medium saucepan and heat on medium heat. Add the sugar and water and mix well. Add the remaining flour and continue to cook and stir until the fruit filling is thickened. Remove the filling from the heat and cool. Spread the fruit filling over half of the cooled cookies and top the filling with the remaining cookies.

Makes 22 servings, 2 cookies each.

🍴

*Calories 248   Total Fat 5 g.   Saturated Fat 3 g.   % Calories from Fat 18
Carbohydrates 49 g.   Protein 3 g.   Cholesterol 31 mg.   Sodium 133 mg.*

Pear Coffee Cake

A delectable and light cake made with juicy Bosc pears.

3	Bosc pears, peeled, cored and quartered
1¼ cups	all-purpose flour
3/4 cup	sugar
1/8 teaspoon	salt
1/4 cup	butter, chilled and cut into small cubes
2 tablespoons	sliced almonds, toasted
1/4 teaspoon	ground cinnamon
1/8 teaspoon	ground nutmeg
1/3 cup	sour cream
1/4 cup	light cream
1 teaspoon	vanilla extract
1/2 teaspoon	baking powder
1/4 teaspoon	baking soda
1 large	egg
	crème fraiche for garnish

Following the owner's manual directions, attach the mixing arm and place the pears in the food tray. Set the time for steam and automatic mash for 35-40 minutes, or until the pears are tender.

Preheat oven to 350°F. Coat a 9-inch cake pan with cooking spray. In a large bowl combine the flour, sugar and salt and stir well with a whisk. Using a pastry blender, cut the butter into the flour until the mixture is the consistency of small peas. Remove 1/3 of the crumbs, place them in a small bowl and stir in the almonds, cinnamon and nutmeg. Set aside.

To the two-thirds crumbs, add the sour cream, cream, vanilla, baking powder, baking soda and egg. Beat with an electric mixer until smooth. Fold in the mashed pears. Pour the batter into the prepared pan and sprinkle the top with the remaining almond crumbs. Bake for 45 minutes or until cake tester comes out clean. Cool the cake completely on a wire rack.

Makes 8 servings.

❧❦

Calories 298   Total Fat 11 g.   Saturated Fat 6 g.   % Calories from Fat 33
Carbohydrates 47 g.   Protein 4 g.   Cholesterol 55 mg.   Sodium 120 mg.

Cinnamon & Pecan Cake

Surprisingly, squash makes this cake moist and tender!

Cake:

1 small	acorn squash, peeled and quartered
1/4 cup	butter, softened
3/4 cup	light brown sugar, firmly packed
1 large	egg
1/2 teaspoon	vanilla extract
2 cups	all-purpose flour
2 teaspoons	baking soda
1/2 teaspoon	salt
1 teaspoon	ground cinnamon
1 cup	pecans, chopped

Cinnamon & Pecan Streusel Topping:

1/2 cup	light brown sugar
1/3 cup	all-purpose flour
1/2 teaspoon	ground cinnamon
1/4 cup	butter, softened
1/2 cup	pecans, chopped
	vanilla ice cream for garnish

Following the owner's manual directions, attach the mixing arm and place the squash in the food tray. Set the timer to steam and automatic mash for 30-40 minutes, or until the squash is tender. Set aside to cool.

Preheat the oven to 350°F. Lightly coat a 9-inch round cake pan with cooking spray. In a large bowl, beat together the butter and sugar until light and creamy. Add the egg, beating well. Stir in 1 cup mashed squash and the vanilla. In a separate bowl, stir together the flour, baking soda, salt and cinnamon. Add the dry ingredients gradually to the squash batter. Stir in the pecans and pour the batter into the prepared pan

In a small bowl, mix together the *Cinnamon & Pecan Streusel Topping*. Crumble the topping over the cake batter. Bake for 40 minutes or until a cake tester inserted in the center of the cake comes out clean. Cool the cake on a wire rack. To serve, cut into individual pieces and top each with a scoop of vanilla ice cream

Makes 9 servings.

🍴

Calories 373   Total Fat 21 g.   Saturated Fat 5 g.   % Calories from Fat 48
Carbohydrates 44 g.   Protein 6 g.   Cholesterol 39 mg.   Sodium 421 mg.

Sweet Peaches Ice Cream

This ice cream will disappear quickly.
so make plenty for everyone.

1 pound	ripe peaches, peeled, halved and pitted
2 cups	sugar, divided
1½ tablespoons	fresh squeezed lemon juice
4	eggs, slightly beaten
1/4 teaspoon	salt
2 quarts	whole milk, divided
1 pint	heavy whipping cream, partially whipped
1/4 teaspoon	vanilla extract

Following the owner's manual directions, attach the mixing arm and place the peaches in the food tray. Set the timer for steam and automatic mash for 35-45 minutes, or until the peaches are tender. Spoon the peaches into a small bowl. Add one cup sugar and lemon juice and mix well. Cover with plastic wrap and set aside for 1 hour.

In a non-reactive double boiler, add the remaining sugar and the salt to the beaten eggs. Blend in half of the milk. Place the boiler over boiling water and cook and stir until a thick custard is formed. Remove from the heat and cool. Add the remaining milk, the partially whipped cream, vanilla and the peach pulp to the custard and mix well to blend. Freeze according to the ice cream maker directions.

Makes 10 servings.

¶|¶

*Calories 507 Total Fat 28 g. Saturated Fat 16 g. % Calories from Fat 48
Carbohydrates 56 g. Protein 11 g. Cholesterol 183 mg. Sodium 198 mg.*

White Chocolate Macadamia Chews

The name of this candy says it all—delicious!

2 medium	russet potatoes, peeled and cubed
1 pound	powdered sugar
1 1/2 teaspoon	vanilla extract
1 cup	coconut, shredded
1 cup	macadamia nuts, coarsely chopped
2 cups	white chocolate chips, melted

Following the owner's manual directions, attach the mixing arm and place the potatoes in the food tray. Set the timer to steam and automatic mash for 35-40 minutes, or until the potatoes are tender. Spoon the potatoes into a large mixing bowl and set aside.

To melt the white chocolate chips, place the chips in a self-sealing plastic bag. Place the bag in a pan of hot water. The chocolate will melt slowly.

Add the sugar, vanilla, coconut and macadamia nuts to the mashed potatoes. Stir to completely blend. Spread the candy evenly into a 9 x 13-inch pan that has been lightly coated with cooking spray. Cut a hole in the corner of the white chocolate bag and pour the melted chocolate over the top of the candy. Using a spatula, spread the white chocolate evenly and smoothly. Cover the pan and refrigerate to chill. When the candy is chilled, cut into pieces and refrigerate it in an airtight container for up to 1 week.

Serves 25, 2 candies per serving.

Calories 235   Total Fat 12 g.   Saturated Fat 5 g.   % Calories from Fat 43
Carbohydrates 34 g.   Protein 3 g.   Cholesterol 0 mg.   Sodium 16 mg.

Swirled Chocolate & Cashew Caramels

*Prepared caramel sauce and semi-sweet chocolate chips
are molded into a delicious candy.*

2 medium	russet potatoes, peeled and cubed
2 tablespoons	lowfat milk
1 pound	powdered sugar
1½ teaspoons	vanilla extract
1/2 cup	caramel sauce
1 cup	semi-sweet chocolate chips
1 tablespoon	vegetable oil
1/2 cup	cashews, finely chopped

Following the owner's manual directions, attach the mixing arm and place the potatoes in the food tray. Set the timer to steam and automatic mash for 35-40 minutes, or until the potatoes are tender. When the mashing cycle ends, add the milk and mix until smooth. Spoon the mashed potatoes into a large bowl, cover and cool.

To the cooled potatoes, add the powdered sugar and vanilla and mix until a dough forms. Roll the dough out on a piece of waxed paper to about 1/4-inch thick. Spread the caramel sauce over the dough evenly. In a small saucepan over low heat, heat the chocolate chips and oil together until warm. Drizzle over the caramel. Sprinkle the chopped cashews over the chocolate and roll the candy as a jelly roll. Cover the candy roll tightly with wax paper or plastic wrap and refrigerate until it is chilled. Slice thinly and serve.

Serves 25, 2 candies per serving.

෴

Calories 158   Total Fat 4 g.   Saturated Fat 2 g.   % Calories from Fat 23
Carbohydrates 31 g.   Protein 1 g.   Cholesterol <1 mg.   Sodium 35 mg.

Chocolate & Walnut Fudge Squares

Rich, rich chocolate fudge, with or without the walnuts.

1/2 pound	russet potatoes, peeled and cubed
2 tablespoons	lowfat milk
1/4 cup	butter, softened
1½ pounds	powdered sugar
6 1-ounce	squares cooking chocolate, melted
pinch	salt
1/2 cup	walnuts, chopped

Following the owner's manual directions, attach the mixing arm and place the potatoes into the food tray. Set the timer to steam and automatic mash for 35-40 minutes, or until the potatoes are tender. When the mashing cycle ends, add the milk and use the mix button to pulse until smooth. Spoon the potatoes into a large mixing bowl, cover and cool.

Add the butter and sugar to the potatoes and mix well. Add the melted chocolate and the salt and combine thoroughly. Stir in the walnuts. Spoon the fudge into a 9 x 13-inch pan that has been coated with cooking spray and spread evenly. Cover and refrigerate until the fudge is chilled. To serve, cut into small pieces.

Serves 25, 2 pieces per serving.

Calories 176   Total Fat 5 g.   Saturated Fat 1 g.   % Calories from Fat 26
Carbohydrates 32 g.   Protein 1 g.   Cholesterol 5 mg.   Sodium 8 mg.

Cinnamon Carrot Muffins

Try these muffins for a lazy day breakfast.

3 small	carrots, peeled and halved
3	eggs
1½ cups	sugar
1/2 cup	vegetable oil
1½ teaspoons	vanilla extract
2½ cups	flour
2 teaspoons	baking soda
1/2 teaspoon	salt
2 teaspoons	ground cinnamon

Following the owner's manual directions, attach the mixing arm and place the carrots in the food tray. Set the time to steam and automatic mash for 50 minutes, or until the carrots are tender.

Preheat oven to 400°F. Lightly coat a 12 cup muffin pan with cooking spray (or prepare a 6 cup muffin pan, if desired). In a large bowl, whisk together the eggs, sugar, oil and vanilla until well blended. In a separate bowl, combine the flour, baking soda, salt and cinnamon. Add the flour mixture to the egg mixture and stir to combine. Stir in the mashed carrots until fully blended.

Spoon the batter evenly among the prepared muffin cups. Bake the muffins for 20-25 minutes, or until the tops are golden and a cake tester inserted into the middle of a muffin comes out clean. Cool the muffins in the pan on a wire rack for 10 minutes. Transfer the muffins from the pan to the wire rack to cool completely.

Makes 12 medium or 6 large muffins.

🍴

Calories 299 Total Fat 11 g. Saturated Fat 2 g. % Calories from Fat 32
Carbohydrates 47 g. Protein 4 g. Cholesterol 53 mg. Sodium 328 mg.

Cherry Apple Wheat Muffins

*Start with homemade applesauce and add healthful whole wheat
and wheat germ. The results are delicious!*

1 cup	*Perfectly Pure Baby Applesauce* (see recipe p.11)
1/4 cup	liquid egg substitute
3/4 cup	whole wheat flour
1 cup	flour
2 tablespoons	toasted wheat germ
1/2 cup	dark brown sugar
2 teaspoons	baking powder
1 teaspoon	ground cinnamon
1/2 teaspoon	ground nutmeg
3/4 cup	dried cherries

Mix together in a large bowl the applesauce and egg substitute. Add the wheat flour, flour, wheat germ, brown sugar, baking powder, cinnamon and nutmeg and mix just until the ingredients are mixed. Do not over-mix. Stir in the dried cherries.

Preheat the oven to 400°F. Coat a 12-cup muffin tin with cooking spray. Spoon the batter into the prepared muffin cups. Bake for 12 to 15 minutes, or until the muffins are lightly browned. Place the muffin tin on a wire rack to cool for 10 minutes. Remove the muffins from the tin and serve while warm.

Makes 12 muffins.

🍴

Calories 157 Total Fat 4 g. Saturated Fat 1 g. % Calories from Fat 20
Carbohydrates 29 g. Protein 3 g. Cholesterol 0 mg. Sodium 80 mg.

Aromatic Sweet Potato Bread

Fresh thyme makes the difference in this bread.

2 medium	sweet potatoes, peeled and quartered
1 cup	all-purpose flour
1/2 cup	whole wheat flour
2 tablespoons	yellow onion, minced
1¼ teaspoons	baking soda
1/2 teaspoon	salt
1 tablespoon	fresh thyme, minced
1/4 cup	sugar
1/3 cup	vegetable oil
2 large	eggs

Following the owner's manual directions, attach the mixing arm and place the potatoes in the food tray. Set the timer to steam and automatic mash for 35-40 minutes, or until the potatoes are tender.

Preheat oven to 350°F. In a medium bowl, combine the flours, onion, baking soda and salt. Stir well and set aside. In a large bowl, combine the sweet potatoes, sugar, oil, eggs and thyme; mix well. Gradually add in the dry ingredients, stir until blended. Spread the batter evenly in an 8-inch round baking pan that has been coated with cooking spray and bake for 25-30 minutes, or until a cake tester comes out clean. Place the pan on a wire rack to cool slightly. Cut into wedges and serve warm.

Makes 8 servings.

🍴

Calories 240 Total Fat 11 g. Saturated Fat 1 g. % Calories from Fat 40
Carbohydrates 32 g. Protein 5 g. Cholesterol 53 mg. Sodium 363 mg.

California Date Coffee Cake

Moist and chewy cake squares.

3 medium	zucchini squash, peeled and quartered
1 cup	granulated sugar
1/2 cup	butter or margarine, softened
1/4 cup	buttermilk
1/2 cup	sour cream
2 large	eggs
1/2 cup	dates, pitted and chopped
3 cups	all-purpose flour
1 teaspoon	baking soda
1/2 teaspoon	salt
6 tablespoons	all-purpose flour
6 tablespoons	packed brown sugar
1/4 cup	cold butter or margarine, cut into small pieces

Following the owner's manual directions, attach the mixing arm and place the zucchini in the food tray. Set the timer to steam and automatic mash for 15-20 minutes, or until the zucchini are tender. Set aside to cool.

Preheat the oven to 350°F. Lightly coat a 9-inch square baking dish with cooking spray and dust with flour. In a large bowl, combine the sugar and softened butter. Beat with an electric mixer until light and fluffy, about 2 minutes. Add the buttermilk and sour cream and blend well. Add the eggs, one at a time, beating well after each addition. Add the cooled zucchini and the chopped dates and mix on low speed. In a separate bowl, combine the 3 cups of flour, baking soda and salt and mix well. Add the flour mixture to the sugar mixture and combine thoroughly. Spoon the batter into the prepared baking dish.

In a small bowl, combine the 6 tablespoons of flour and the brown sugar. Cut in the chilled butter with a pastry blender until coarse crumbs form. Sprinkle the crumb mixture over the cake batter and bake for 35 minutes, or until a cake tester inserted in the center of the cake comes out clean. Serve warm.

Makes 12 servings.

🍴

Calories 385 Total Fat 15 g. Saturated Fat 2 g. % Calories from Fat 35
Carbohydrates 58 g. Protein 6 g. Cholesterol 72 mg. Sodium 228 mg.

Potato Pancakes Topped with Warm Ricotta Apricot Sauce

*Serve these small pancakes as you would crepes—
for an elegant finish.*

1 pound	russet potatoes, peeled and cubed
1/4 cup	lowfat milk
2 tablespoons	all-purpose flour
1/4 teaspoon	salt
1/8 teaspoon	ground white pepper
1 teaspoon	ground nutmeg
2	eggs, lightly beaten (use egg substitute, if desired)
2 tablespoons	lowfat milk
1/2 cup	lowfat margarine

Ricotta Apricot Sauce:

1 cup	ricotta cheese
1/4 cup	lowfat milk
1 teaspoon	lemon juice
1 cup	apricot preserves

Following the owner's manual directions, attach the mixing arm and place the potatoes in the food tray. Set the timer to steam and automatic mash for 35-40 minutes, or until the potatoes are tender. Add the milk to the mashed potatoes and use the mix button to pulse until smooth.

In a large bowl, combine the flour, salt, pepper and nutmeg. Add the eggs and milk and beat until smooth. Stir in the potatoes and mix well. In a large skillet over medium heat, melt the margarine and drop rounded spoonfuls of the batter into the margarine. Flatten the batter with a spatula, and fry until crisp and golden on both sides. Serve hot from the skillet with the *Warm Ricotta Apricot Sauce.*

Makes 4 servings.

♈︎

Warm Ricotta Apricot Sauce:

In a saucepan over low heat, combine the cheese, milk and the lemon juice. Stir until the sauce is heated through. Remove the sauce from the heat and add the apricot preserves. Mix well until blended.

Makes 2 cups.

♈︎

Calories 457 Total Fat 18 g. Saturated Fat 8 g. % Calories from Fat 33 Carbohydrates 66 g. Protein 15 g. Cholesterol 134 mg. Sodium 546 mg.

Autumn Pancakes

Perfect for a crowd of hungry breakfast seekers!

1/2 pound	pumpkin, seeded and cubed
1/4 cup	heavy cream
1 tablespoon	butter
1 tablespoon	sugar
1½ cups	whole wheat flour
2 teaspoons	baking powder
1 teaspoon	pumpkin pie spice
1/4 teaspoon	salt
2	eggs, separated
1 cup	lowfat milk
2 teaspoons	butter, melted
	maple syrup

Following the owner's manual directions, place the pumpkin in the food tray and set the timer to steam for 40-45 minutes, or until the pumpkin is tender. Allow the pumpkin to cool slightly. Remove the pulp from the shell and place the pulp in the food tray. Discard the shell. Attach the mixing arm and mash until the pumpkin is smooth. When the mashing cycle ends, add the cream, butter and sugar and use the mix button to pulse until smooth. Spoon the pumpkin puree into a large bowl, cover and cool.

In a separate bowl, sift together the flour, baking powder, pumpkin pie spice and salt. When the pumpkin puree has cooled, beat in the egg yolks, milk and butter. Add the dry ingredients and mix well. In a small bowl, beat the egg whites until stiff peaks form. Fold the egg whites into the pumpkin batter.

Lightly coat a skillet with cooking spray and heat over medium heat. Spoon 1/4 cup of the batter onto the hot skillet and fry until both sides of the pancake are golden brown. Serve immediately with hot maple syrup.

Makes 4 servings.

🍴

Calories 344   Total Fat 15 g.   Saturated Fat 5 g.   % Calories from Fat 38
Carbohydrates 43 g.   Protein 12 g.   Cholesterol 144 mg.   Sodium 416 mg.

Cinnamon Crepes with Cream Filling

Similar to Italian canoli dessert rolls, these crepes are for special occasions.

Cream Filling:

1/2 pound	sweet potatoes, peeled and cubed
2 tablespoons	light cream
1/4 cup	butter
1/4 cup	sugar
2 tablespoons	cream cheese
2 tablespoons	sour cream
2	egg yolks
1½ teaspoons	vanilla extract
2 teaspoons	orange zest

Following the owner's manual directions, attach the mixing arm and place the sweet potatoes in the food tray. Set the timer to steam and automatic mash for 35-40 minutes, or until the potatoes are tender. When the mashing cycle ends, add the cream and use the mix button to pulse until smooth. Spoon the mashed potatoes into a large mixing bowl, cover and cool.

In a separate bowl, cream together the butter and sugar and add to the cooled sweet potatoes. Add the cream cheese, sour cream, egg yolks and orange zest to the potatoes and beat until fluffy. Place the filling in a piping bag with a large tip. Pipe the filling into the hot crepes and roll.

Crepes:

3	eggs, lightly beaten
1/2 cup	all-purpose flour
1/2 teaspoon	vanilla extract
1 tablespoon	sugar
1/2 teaspoon	ground cinnamon
1/2 cup	lowfat milk

Combine all of the crepe ingredients in a large bowl. Use an electric mixer on high speed to blend until the consistency is like thick cream. If the batter is too thick, add more milk, or if it is too thin, add more flour. Coat a large sauté pan with cooking spray and heat over medium-high heat. Pour 1/4 cup batter into the pan and quickly spread it evenly over the bottom of the pan by lifting and swirling the pan. Cook until both sides are golden brown. Place the crepe on a plate, pipe in the *Cream Filling* and serve immediately.

Makes 4 servings.

🍴

*Calories 454   Total Fat 26 g.   Saturated Fat 7 g.   % Calories from Fat 52
Carbohydrates 44 g.   Protein 8 g.   Cholesterol 321 mg.   Sodium 84 mg.*

Cinnamon & Spice Donuts

Down-home goodness in every bite.

1/2 pound	russet potatoes, peeled and cubed
2 tablespoons	lowfat milk
1½ teaspoons	salt, divided
2	eggs
1/4 cup	lowfat milk
2 tablespoons	butter, melted
2/3 cup	sugar
2½ cups	all-purpose flour
4 teaspoons	baking powder
1 teaspoon	ground nutmeg
1/2 teaspoon	ground allspice
	oil for deep frying
1 teaspoon	ground cinnamon
2 tablespoons	sugar

Following the owner's manual directions, attach the mixing arm and place the potatoes into the food tray. Set the timer to steam and automatic mash for 35-40 minutes, or until the potatoes are tender. When the mashing cycle ends, add 2 tablespoons milk and 1 teaspoon salt and use the mix button to pulse until smooth. Cool to room temperature.

Spoon the cooled potatoes into a large mixing bowl and add the eggs, 1/4 cup milk, butter and sugar and mix well. In a separate bowl, sift together the flour, baking powder, remaining salt, nutmeg and allspice. Slowly add the dry ingredients to the potatoes, mixing thoroughly. The batter will be soft and sticky. Cover and chill until the dough can be handled easily, about 1 hour.

On a lightly floured surface, roll the dough out to 3/4-inch thick. Cut out the donuts with a large circular cookie cutter or cup. Cut out the center of each donut. In a 4-quart saucepan, heat 2 inches of oil to 375°F. Drop the donuts into the hot oil and cook for 2-3 minutes or until golden. The donuts will initially sink and then float to the top as they fry. Place the fried donuts on a plate lined with paper towels. You may also fry the donut holes for quick bites. In a small bowl, combine the cinnamon and sugar and sprinkle over the hot donuts. Serve while warm.

Serves 18, 1 donut each.

🍴

Calories 121   Total Fat 2 g.   Saturated Fat <1 g.   % Calories from Fat 16
Carbohydrates 23 g.   Protein 3 g.   Cholesterol 27 mg.   Sodium 293 mg.

Index

Index

Index